"I fell in love with black; it contained all colours. It wasn't a negation of colour ... Black is the most aristocratic colour of all ... You can be quiet, and it contains the whole thing."

—LOUISE NEVELSON, AMERICAN SCULPTOR

SUSAN REDMAN

MODERN HOUSES IN BLACK

This book is dedicated to all architects, designers and artists who create beauty with the colour black.

CONTENTS

10	Introduction: The Beauty of Black Houses		
13	AER House | France	149	Granary House | Portugal
23	Ardmore House | United States	159	Iron Chef | Australia
31	Birdhouse | Lithuania	169	Lubowsee House | Germany
41	Black Timber House | United Kingdom	179	Murakoshi House | Japan
51	Bromelia Retreat | Costa Rica	187	N House | South Korea
61	CH73 House | Mexico	195	Olive Passive House | United States
73	Casa BB | Chile	205	Perforated House | Singapore
81	The Coast House | New Zealand	215	Plover House | United States
89	Columbia River Valley Lookout | Canada	223	Qingli House | China
99	Dutch Barn | United Kingdom	231	Rockham House | United Kingdom
109	Dutchess County Studio | United States	241	Sandringham House | Australia
119	Everden House | Canada	249	Taigh na Tràigh | United Kingdom
127	Federal House | Australia	259	Villa Backyard | Thailand
139	Floating Home | The Netherlands	267	Villa Timmerman | Sweden
		276	Project Credits
		279	About the Author

Introduction

THE BEAUTY OF BLACK HOUSES

A black house commands attention. Black adds drama, sophistication and edginess to contemporary residential architecture. Like black designer fashion, a black house requires few embellishments to impress, and often makes a bold statement by simply focusing on form and structure.

In the urban context, a black house often provides a welcome contrast to an otherwise drab streetscape and, depending on the form it takes, can immediately suggest a place of refuge and sanctuary. In a rural setting, a black dwelling can either stand out from its surroundings, depending on whether it is sited on a hill or on a wide open plain, or blend in, if nestled deep in a forest or jungle. Additionally, the façades of a black house, provide perfect backdrops to gardens and landscaping.

In this book *Modern Houses in Black*, the trend in black house design is explored by presenting 28 recently built residential projects sited in both urban and rural locations and found in 19 countries across the world. Illustrated by stunning photography, the projects are accompanied by interviews with architects to examine why the houses featured are black, and how this has been achieved.

Historically, the designers of residential architecture avoided dark exteriors, but due to the influence of Japanese and Scandinavian architects who challenged design conventions in the early 2000s by experimenting with daring black forms built with an unorthodox use of materials, many architects today have developed an appreciation of black exteriors. Two decades on, this trend in black house design continues to evolve. These developments are the focus of this book *Modern Houses in Black*, which features projects completed since 2020.

One recent manifestation is in elevating the elegance black lends to an architectural project while dialling down the daring. This has resulted in house shapes that have become less offbeat in form while enveloping interiors that are less stark.

A black exterior is also a great choice for modern homes requiring protection from the elements, while simultaneously providing a striking aesthetic. For example, black metal cladding is often applied to the exterior of a house, and sometimes wrapped over the roof, to provide a sleek, industrial look, as well as offering a durable, low-maintenance finish.

Due to the superior robustness and timelessness of brick, a housing material that can protect inhabitants from high temperatures and exposure to harsh weather conditions, architects are increasingly re-evaluating its use in contemporary architecture. By choosing to build with black bricks and roof tiles, featuring either a matte or glazed finish, a black house can display both a contemporary aesthetic while ensuring the structure's stability.

Similarly, black concrete is emerging as a material of choice for the exterior exoskeleton of residential architecture. This is especially true for those that might require an unusual form, since concrete can be poured and moulded into shapes. A black tint is added to the concrete mix to give the exterior of the home a groomed, often monolithic, appearance.

Architects often opt for black-stained or painted timber siding, panelling or screens to provide textural details to an otherwise stark black façade. From a visual perspective, black timber slats, battens or planks can be arranged and layered to create various distinctive patterns—horizontal, vertical or diagonal—resulting in an understated yet elegant surface.

By far, one of the most remarkable and unique methods to blacken the exteriors of the modern home is to apply a heat-treatment to pre-cut timbers. Japanese woodworkers call it *yakisugi* but it is also referred to in the West as Shou Sugi Ban. The technique, however, is generally the same: a direct flame chars purpose-cut planks of wood, which are typically cypress or cedar, and these are then used to clad the building.

Houses clad, stained and screened in black are also great options for those architects looking to create homes that are energy efficient, as the dark colour helps to absorb and retain heat, leading to lower utility costs. This is especially beneficial in countries that experience cold winters. However, some architects are challenging this notion by designing black homes for warmer climes. By using black outer skeletons that include screens, acutely angled roof lines, often combined with perforations and open ventilation, a black house in a tropical environment can reduce glare and merge into its surroundings, offering a shady respite within.

While a black house is not for everyone, the 28 projects featured in this book will no doubt appeal to lovers of distinctive design, and especially to those who appreciate both the daring and sophistication that black offers residential architecture.

Susan Redman

I acknowledge the First Nations people of the land on which the houses in this book are built. I also pay my respects to the Gadigal and Wangal people of the Eora Nation in Australia, the traditional custodians of the land on which I live and work.

Onesse-Laharie, France

AER HOUSE

Borrowing from the aesthetics of agricultural barns found on large grassy fields in southwest France, AER House has been designed as an elegant yet simple dwelling. Classic workshed features have been translated into sophisticated elements. These are most notable in the wooden frame, wide external doors, large sliding shutters and a shed or skillion roof with deep, overhanging eaves.

The structure was designed by architecture firm Lesgourgues primarily as a holiday home for clients who desired to come together with family and friends in a rural location, specifically in Onesse-Laharie in the Landes region.

Considering the home's purpose, lead architect Emmanuelle Lesgourgues placed emphasis on creating a spacious communal area at ground level, where gatherings and activities could easily transition from indoors to outside. "For this purpose, a wide concrete border surrounds the building and acts as a terrace, with large ground floor doors opening directly onto this space," she says.

To aid this movement and to increase the connection to the surrounding countryside, Lesgourgues also positioned two very wide, barn-like door openings opposite each other in the living room. "It makes this entire area neither-inside-or-outside space, but a covered space where it is possible to shelter from the rain and the sun," says Lesgourgues.

Shelter on the terrace outside is provided by 2-metre-wide (6-foot-wide) cantilevered asymmetric eaves. "These prevent the south-western rays from reaching the house," says Lesgourgues. "Coupled with the ventilation of the facing open door bays, the central space promises a certain coolness, especially in the summer."

Clad in Douglas fir pine treated with black tar, the house is immediately noticeable across the open green meadow of the property. Huge sliding shutters featuring blackened wood claustra-work lattice cover the large openings, filtering light throughout the day. They also thwart possible animal intrusions at night, while allowing the house to be naturally ventilated at all times.

Clad in Douglas fir pine treated with black tar, the house is immediately noticeable across the open green meadow of the property.

Inside AER House, the living area is a double-height space that includes the kitchen, living room and a black iron stove for heating. Also on this ground floor level is a master bedroom, a dressing room, a bathroom and a utility room. These are positioned behind a central staircase, made from pale knotty pine, which incorporates built-in storage. The stairs lead to an upper floor where there are two more bedrooms and a bathroom.

Ever mindful of incorporating opportunities to view the natural environment, Lesgourgues ensured the windows of all three bedrooms were generous enough to frame significant views of the nearby forest. Timber shutters neatly fit over their large square frames, further securing the house when it is in lock-up and the family departs.

"Coupled with the ventilation of the facing open door bays, the central space promises a certain coolness, especially in the summer."

—EMMANUELLE LESGOURGUES

Chicago, Illinois, United States

ARDMORE HOUSE

Designed by Kwong Von Glinow and located on a typical Chicago block at the intersection of a residential street and an alleyway, Ardmore House is a single-family home built to showcase the design talents of Alison Von Glinow and Lap Chi Kwong. The couple created the sophisticated dwelling as their private residence and, in doing so, proved it's possible to design a high-quality home for a standard city lot.

Pushing the built envelope to the edge of the plot, the architects flipped a typical floor plan of a two-storey house, placing the bedrooms of Ardmore House on the lower level and communal spaces on the floor above. In this way, the living areas benefitted from additional natural light gained through windows on all four sides.

"This approach supports contemporary ways of living, emphasising communal areas, interconnectivity and flexible live-work spaces that receive ample natural light and engage the surrounding urban context," says Alison Von Glinow.

Ardmore House has a simple, vernacular form, with a rectangular footprint and a standard pitched roof. It rests on a concrete base punctuated by the windows of a partially sunken basement, which was designed to serve a variety of purposes, incorporating an office space, storage room and an independently accessible self-contained rental.

The exterior of the house is clad in Accoya wood, which on the first level is half grey and black—the latter shade extending up to cover the second storey as well.

"This approach to the use of exterior materials emphasises the sectional flip and lends visual rhythm to the dark monolithic building," says Von Glinow. "The result is a house that engages the neighbourhood's traditional vernacular style while reflecting the organisation of the interior spaces at each level."

Kwong says they included another 'flip' in the design of the façade in order to "shift the focus of the façade hierarchy away from the street to the alleyway". This was achieved by reducing openings on the street-facing façade—there is just a row of half-height ribbon windows along the second floor and only a single opaque door on the first level to maintain privacy for the front bedroom. On the alleyway side, however, a 17-metre-long (56-foot-long) ribbon of floor-to-ceiling windows run the entire length of the second storey. Additionally, a large picture window faces out to the alleyway from the interior courtyard, opening the home's interior to the urban surroundings.

The single-most distinctive characteristic of the home's interior layout is a curving double-height courtyard atrium. It extends longitudinally from the front to rear doors, doubling as a hallway. While its openness promotes ventilation throughout the home, this quality also establishes a vertical link between the communal areas on the first and second levels. "The internal atrium offers an informal multipurpose area where residents can relax and children can play," says Von Glinow.

"This approach to the use of exterior materials emphasises the sectional flip and lends visual rhythm to the dark grey and black monolithic building."
—ALISON VON GLINOW

On the first level, doors to the home's three bedrooms, and their en suite bathrooms, are positioned along the atrium's curved wall. Tucked behind it, a staircase leads to the open-plan second storey, which has been divided up into five zones defined by functionality: a kitchen, an island benchtop, the dining area, a powder room and a lounge room. Each 'zone' is visually segmented by four large wooden ceiling trusses, which are on dramatic view overhead, and also hold the timber-framed house together.

To create a sense of serenity inside, the interiors feature a restrained colour and material palette of white walls complemented by white oak wood floors, trusses and furnishings.

"All of the shared and public spaces on the second floor are oriented towards the ribbon window that spans the length of the interior courtyard and floods the home with natural light," says Lap Chi Kwong. "This offers panoramic views that capture the fullness of the surrounding neighbourhood: beautiful century-old trees, the back balconies and fire-escapes of neighbouring buildings and street lamps with their meandering cabling. The combination of old and new make it a great place to live."

"All of the shared and public spaces on the second floor are oriented towards the ribbon window that spans the length of the interior courtyard and floods the home with natural light, offering panoramic views that capture the fullness of the surrounding neighbourhood."

—LAP CHI KWONG

Vilnius, Lithuania

BIRDHOUSE

Situated in a bustling neighbourhood of older and established private homes in Vilnius, the capital of Lithuania, stands an angular two-storey residence with a one-car garage designed by local architectural firm, YCL studio. This modern abode not only features a striking black wooden exterior but it is also distinguished by a large, round window high on the northern façade—reminiscent of a birdhouse.

To further individualise the sculptural form of the house, the architectural team added a number of vertical, mirrored details across the walls of the inky black exterior.

"This provided an understated illusion of reflecting the always-changing surroundings," says one of the three lead architects, Aidas Barzda. "We affixed them to the dark, thermo-wood slatted façade, so that the mirrors would create subtle yet contrasting colour shifts, depending on the time of the day and angle of view," he says.

"The separate garage was designed to create a privacy buffer between the Birdhouse and a neighbouring home," says Barzda, "but to make the garage more visually appealing, we added large, mirrored panels to the structure."

This small but significant light-reflective feature on both the garage and vertical slats works extremely well. In a country as far north as Lithuania, people desire as much light as possible, whether natural or reflective, to brighten their living conditions. To that end, the reflected light bouncing off the garage's mirrored cladding creates the illusion of an extended backyard or a parallel world. Unsurprisingly, the homeowners are delighted with this unexpected feature.

This modern abode not only features a striking black wooden exterior but it is also distinguished by a large, round window high on the northern façade—reminiscent of a birdhouse.

Inside the home, the clients had made a key request of YCL studio to include a large common area for the family to come together.

"The owners didn't want this space divided by stairs in any way, so to achieve this in the design phase, we positioned the stairs just inside the perimeter of the house," says Barzda. "This decision created an interesting housing shape externally, too, producing different views of the residence as one walks around it."

The interior structure of Birdhouse is divided into two levels. The ground floor includes a living area, a guest bathroom, a utility room and a guest bedroom or work room. The upper floor has three bedrooms and two bathrooms, with a void spatially connecting the floors.

The south façade of the house faces the backyard garden. It has a rhythmical window pattern, which helps maintain the monolithic and laconic shape of the 'birdhouse'. Also out back, is a deck area covered by a suspended roof.

"This terrace corresponds to the overall composition of shapes and makes an outdoor family space more inviting, even when it rains," says Barzda.

"Although not imposing in size, the laconic shape of Birdhouse is an easy-to-identify contemporary black structure," Barzda continues, "creating an intriguing path of new residential architecture in a traditional district of older private homes."

"Although not imposing in size, the laconic shape of Birdhouse is an easy-to-identify contemporary black structure, creating an intriguing path of new residential architecture in a traditional district of older private homes."

—AIDAS BARZDA, YCL STUDIO

Rodmell, Sussex, United Kingdom

BLACK TIMBER HOUSE

Nestled in the picturesque South Downs National Park conservation area, Black Timber House is tucked away at the end of a tranquil country lane. Sheltering under large ash trees and surrounded by sweeping wildflower meadows, it is situated on a 1,012-square-metre (0.25-acre) site in Rodmell. This stunning eco house, designed by Sussex architects HAPA, features picture-frame windows that capture views of the rolling fields, providing inhabitants with a sense of peace and serenity.

The vision of HAPA's architect and director, Stuart Paine, was to craft a timeless home using local and sustainable materials and passive energy consumption techniques: "We wanted to create a family home that was striking, contemporary, but also reacted to its surroundings and was environmentally conscious."

Paine says the building performs at a very high thermal and energy-efficiency standard and is able to generate its own power with the help of PV panels. "The focus was to reduce the energy demands by using a high-efficiency air source heat pump coupled with low temperature under floor heating and high thermal mass heat sink floors," he explains. "The house also employs passive solar design, high levels of insulation and air tightness measures to make for an A rated house (A rated EPC)."

The structure of the house incorporates two volumes: a large box topped by a gabled upper storey, which are stacked together to create a protective entry overhang. The verandah and windows expose natural wood, while the rest of the exterior is clad in an impressive charred black timber, using English larch. The timber planks are horizontally affixed to the exterior of the ground-level volume while attached vertically to the one above.

"The black cladding boards create a particularly impressive aesthetic using the *yakisugi* method of charring wood," explains Paine. "This leaves the wood with a highly pronounced grain and greater colour depth. The charring method is also known to improve resistance to moss, algae and insects."

Paine says other materials were selected to patina and weather into the surroundings. "The deep-grain black charred English larch is complemented by natural copper guttering and dark slate roofs to create a feeling of material honesty," he adds.

The black cladding boards create a particularly impressive aesthetic using the *yakisugi* method of charring wood. This leaves the wood with a highly pronounced grain and greater colour depth.

The internal layout was designed with open-plan living in mind. A generous entrance hallway reveals the heart of the home, a large space containing a kitchen, dining and living room. This flows through to a covered terrace with outdoor seating from which to admire the view of the expansive garden and fields beyond.

"Inside, we used surplus engineered oak for the flooring, installed a natural patinated zinc kitchen worktop and other natural products to create an inviting atmosphere," says Paine.

Upstairs, four private bedrooms feature double-height, vaulted ceilings and large windows. "A wrap-over window over the staircase adds fantastic natural light and drama as the occupants climb up towards the canopy space," adds Paine.

Black Timber House showcases impressive energy efficiency, providing its inhabitants with a connection to nature and a sense of wellbeing. Its dark exterior contrasts with the light interiors, with the first floor boasting high ceilings created by its gabled roof. Additionally, the walls are finished with a pale plaster, creating a soothing atmosphere.

"We wanted to create a family home that was striking, contemporary, but also reacted to its surroundings and was environmentally conscious."

Barva de Heredia, Costa Rica

BROMELIA RETREAT

Just north of the capital of Costa Rica, San Jose, sits the long-extinct volcano of Barva. It is there on its slopes that city-based architectural firm Plup! Studio Costa Rica was commissioned to design a small family retreat.

The tropical jungle on the site is nourished by a wet and warm climate, where rainfall is a constant. This presented lead architect on the project, Carlos Andres Bolaños Alfaro, with both a challenge and inspiration for the structure's design.

"The site is an area that presents rain or at least constant spray throughout the year, with an average temperature of 17°C (62°F) and high humidity," says Alfaro.

In order to allow water to drain away, without pooling on the roof or around the home, Alfaro looked to a species of native Bromeliads for inspiration. "The concept and shape of the project is born from the place, from an epiphyte known as bromeliad. These plants live on logs or rocks that function as hosts, and their tank-like shape allows them to capture matter and water for their vital functioning."

By inverting this concept, so that rainfall quickly evacuated, two acutely angled corrugated metal walls were joined at their apex by skylights.

"This shape allows the natural run-off water to fall to the ground and continue on its way. In addition, it allows a correct ventilation of the mezzanine levels within which helps to control humidity," says Alfaro. "This controlled cross ventilation has been coupled with a skylight, which allows the entry of light and, in addition to marking the time, also reduces humidity."

Two almost identical longitudinal structures were built on the site, each with a slightly different floor plan. The family's building contains a mezzanine for the owner and two bedrooms on the lower level, and also enjoys a contemporary kitchen, living and dining arranged in open-planned zones on the main level. The other building was built as a communal space exclusively for hosting guests. It features an expansive, double-height living and dining space.

Each building, however, has large openings at either end of their lean-to like forms, to promote natural cross-ventilation throughout the interiors, especially in the living spaces. When the weather is dry, the skylights can be opened to allow for vertical airflow. Presenting further comfort and amenity, an elevated and recessed sheltered terrace just off the living room provides residents with an outdoor relaxation zone and vantage point to peer out at the surrounding treetops.

The dramatic shapes of Bromelia Retreat are matched by their distinctive black colour. Featuring on external corrugated planes and exposed structural metal framework, the black colouring has the additional benefit of 'hiding' the structures, which appear to blend into the thicket of lush foliage onsite.

While the acute angles of the frames allow for vertical space and height to accommodate living and sleeping quarters, Alfaro says stability and support is achieved by resting the structures on "two concrete service cores". These have been placed in centre position on the sides of each property, and cleverly conceal bathrooms and staircases.

"The use of low-maintenance materials in these simple and inexpensive structures will allow Bromelia Retreat to mature in conjunction within their context in the forest," says Alfaro.

> "The concept and shape of the project is born from the place, from an epiphyte known as bromeliad. These plants live on logs or rocks that function as hosts, and their tank-like shape allows them to capture matter and water for their vital functioning."
>
> —CARLOS ANDRES BOLAÑOS ALFARO

The dramatic shapes of Bromelia Retreat are matched by their distinctive black colour ... 'hiding' the structures, which appear to blend into the thicket of lush foliage on-site.

Bosques de las Lomas, Mexico City, Mexico

CH73 HOUSE

Breaking the paradigms of construction in the area of Bosques de las Lomas in Mexico City, CH73 House is a spectacular cantilevered structure designed by the architectural firm LBR&A to take advantage of the surrounding natural wooded terrain.

"The presence of a federal reserve to the east, the pre-existence of a retaining wall, the adherence to the regulations and the project program itself, all helped us with the architectural design of CH73, conceptualising it as a diaphanous form in cantilever," says lead designer Benjamín Romano.

The 1,023-square-metre (11,011-square-foot), three-bedroom, family residence is built on a steel frame, allowing for a 20-metre (66-foot) cantilever that commands stunning views over the ravine below it.

"The use of steel was driven by the natural cantilever performance," says Romano. "To enhance this, we decided to apply a dark wax patina to the steel structural elements, which would encourage good aging behaviour."

The building's foundation rests on three black concrete load-bearing walls that make up the basement, which includes some living areas and a garage. In turn, the walls are founded on geothermal piles that are used to generate resource savings and, aided by a solar-powered heat pump, work to heat the house in winter and preheat the pool.

"It's important to clarify that the use of geothermal and solar energy allows the house to maintain a 22°C (72°F) temperature all year round, at any time, with zero cost and pollution," says Romano. "The project also includes the installation of a 'biodigester' system to treat wastewater and irrigate the federal zone, as well as water infiltration into the subsoil to promote the growth of flora and fauna original to the site."

"The use of steel was driven by the natural cantilever performance. To intensify this, we decided to apply a dark wax patina to the steel structural elements, which would encourage good aging behaviour."

—BENJAMÍN ROMANO

Romano says that when newly implemented ecological plantings mature, the residential house will be encircled by both the current trees and future greenery.

"As part of the reforestation, and in addition to other trees that had grown naturally on the pre-existing and abandoned platform of the property, it was decided to plant endemic species such as Tepozán, Pino Moctezuma (Ocote) and Aguacateros trees specifically to encourage domestic fauna and help restore the original ecosystem," he says. "We were very excited to learn that a Cacomistle (an endangered racoon-like animal) was recently spotted in the federal zone."

While the exterior façades of CH73 House are both protected and ventilated, with huge sheets of glass providing dramatic views at every step along the cantilevered main floor, the interior spaces are designed to be flexible and adaptable to the changing needs of the occupants. In addition to the three bedrooms, kitchen and bathrooms, the floor plans include numerous relaxing and study zones, a terrace at the end of the cantilever, garaging for two cars, an indoor pool at basement level as well as luxuriant gardens and a private outdoor living area.

"To enhance the views, I used grey and black colours inside the house," says Romano of the design ethos used to create a dramatic yet refined level of modernism employed throughout the home's interior décor. "This palette also serves to maximise the impact of the vivid colours of the family's art collection," he says.

The resulting interior is calm and open, infiltrated by an abundance of light, natural air and open and protected views. "This provides a high quality of life for those living in the house," says Romano.

"To enhance the views, I used grey and black colours inside the house. This palette also serves to maximise the impact of the vivid colours of the family's art collection."

—BENJAMÍN ROMANO

Lake Calafquén, Los Ríos, Chile

CASA BB

Perched atop stilts on a hillside in southern Chile is Casa BB, a black holiday home designed by Chilean architecture studio Elton Léniz. The two-storey structure overlooks serene Lake Calafquén, with the active volcano Villarrica visible in the distance.

"The design maximises unobstructed views of the impressive geography while freeing up as much space as possible between a few neighbouring buildings," says architect and co-founder of the practice Mauricio Léniz.

To minimise any impact on the natural environment and to protect the house from ground moisture, the dwelling was raised up on timber supports. "The result is a compact house that sits almost like a container resting on a wooden structure, with minimal interference to the land and its slope," says Léniz.

The façade of Casa BB is clad in Quadroline aluminium panels, a low-maintenance material with simple, vertical lines. "The black colour helps the home blend into the shadows of the landscape and protects the wooden structures and interior cladding from rainy weather," says architect and co-founder Mirene Elton.

On the north side of the dwelling, an expansive micro-perforated screen provides protection from the sun while still providing a visual connection to the outdoors. Cutouts and openings in the structure also allow occupants to observe the lake, sky and landscape from various viewpoints.

A wooden walkway on the south side leads to the front door. This entry level contains a kitchen, living room, dining area, a sheltered verandah for outdoor barbecue dining, as well as a bedroom. "The social spaces are developed with an open plan to allow simultaneous activities," says Léniz. "The main bedrooms are located on the upper level, protecting the privacy and silence of the inhabitants."

In addition to the 'open-plan design' of the house, Léniz says the contemporary décor and use of natural materials, such as pine, continue to provide a connection to the natural environment outdoors. "This allows one to silently examine the geography and to discover new relations with the landscape from within the space," he says.

"The black colour helps the home blend into the shadows of the landscape and protects the wooden structures and interior cladding from rainy weather."

—MAURICIO LÉNIZ

"The open-plan design allows one to silently examine the geography and to discover new relations with the landscape from within the space."

—MAURICIO LÉNIZ

Omaui, New Zealand

THE COAST HOUSE

Nestled within the windswept coastal beech trees clustered along the wild coast of New Zealand's South Island, is a dark, bunker-like form. This low-energy retreat, the Coast House, is ideally positioned to weather the harsh climate of this remote region, which is located between the Fiordland National Park and the densely forested Catlins—areas renowned for their natural beauty and abundant wildlife.

With a brief to make the most of the rural site and its coastal views, Queenstown-based architect Stacey Farrell designed a modestly sized seaside holiday home, on a very small budget. "My clients wanted a discrete hideaway that was low impact, so the exterior has been prepared for native plants to eventually climb over and conceal it," says Farrell. "The house also had to be able to be locked and left, and used by others when the owners weren't there."

To ensure the home's inhabitants would have panoramic views of Omaui Beach and the mountains of Fiordland, Farrell angled a low-lying structure on the scrubby site to take advantage of its natural slope towards nearby sand dunes and the ocean.

The design comprises two interlocking forms: a long, tapered shape, split to reveal a protected entry, which collides with a larger rectangular black box containing the living quarters.

The first section accommodates a woodshed on one side, storage on the other and, further back, a bedroom. "Once entered, it also provides an airlock to retain heat and give space to remove coats and shoes as the owners seek refuge inside. It also discretely incorporates 'lock and leave' cupboards," says Farrell.

Always considering sustainability values in her projects, Farrell clad the house in corrugated steel sheets, which she says require minimal maintenance and are suitable for rainwater collection. Externally, materials and colours, most notably black and brown, "are deliberately pared back so as not to compete with the natural environment," says Farrell.

Externally, materials and colours, most notably black and brown, are deliberately pared back so as not to compete with the natural environment.

Entry is via the tapered triangular form, which is somewhat compressed, but once inside the larger black-clad form, the house opens up and out to a living area and a second, larger bedroom.

The materials used internally are raw and stripped back. For example, rather than over-lining the Structural Insulated Panels (SIPs) used on the walls, Farrell had them stained and worked with their texture "to add a richness and a lodge-like feel". Elsewhere, ply board linings were used.

After orienting the Coast House for sun, views and heat gain, and complementing exterior and interior choices for materials and colours, Farrell's interior design focused on amenability: "Inside had to feel cosy and luxurious, which is why I incorporated nostalgic elements to reflect traditional Kiwi 'baches' or 'cribs'—small holiday cabins popular in New Zealand," explains Farrell.

"For example, the kitchen is understated, reflecting the client's desire for a holiday feel," says Farrell, "and large, comfortable sofas anchor the relaxing zone. It's from here you access a patio to bird-watch and take in those sweeping ocean views."

"Inside had to feel cosy and luxurious, which is why I incorporated nostalgic elements to reflect traditional Kiwi 'baches' or 'cribs'—small holiday cabins popular in New Zealand."

—STACEY FARRELL

Golden, British Columbia, Canada

COLUMBIA RIVER VALLEY LOOKOUT

Nestled away in the Kootenay mountain range in British Columbia, Canada, is a compact three-storey cabin, purpose-built and designed for family ski holidays. Apart from enjoying deep snowfalls in winter, the Columbia River Valley Lookout also boasts year-round panoramic views of the nearby river, wetlands and forests.

Designing the cabin was a family project. Homeowner Sandra Bassett employed her sister and brother-in-law of Twobytwo Architecture Studio to create a three-bedroom cabin where their family could gather, relax and partake in their favourite winter activities. Sandra's sister Jennifer Bassett took on the role of lead designer while Jennifer's husband David Tyl was the project architect.

The structural design was left to Sandra's husband Chris Urbinsky, whose background in steel fabrication became the primary inspiration for features showcased throughout the cabin. "These features include a third-storey cantilevered black powder-coated steel balcony, which wraps the front and side elevations, a fireplace insert with matching black steel surround and integrated millwork and an industrial staircase with wooden treads that spans the cabin's three levels," lists Jennifer Bassett.

The black metal details inside are complemented externally by a black-stained exterior timber siding. "Black allows the house to integrate into the forest backdrop in the summer and provide a contrast to the blanket of snow during winter months," says Bassett.

Capped with a simple shed or skillion roof to maximise height and openness towards the prevailing views, the cabin's multilevel tall elevation has ensured that the footprint at its base would be modest and thereby cause the least amount of disturbance on the existing plateau. Bassett and Tyl also strategically situated the cabin on-site to optimise sunlight to flow into the interior.

"Black allows the house to integrate into the forest backdrop in the summer and provide a contrast to the blanket of snow during winter months."
—JENNIFER BASSETT

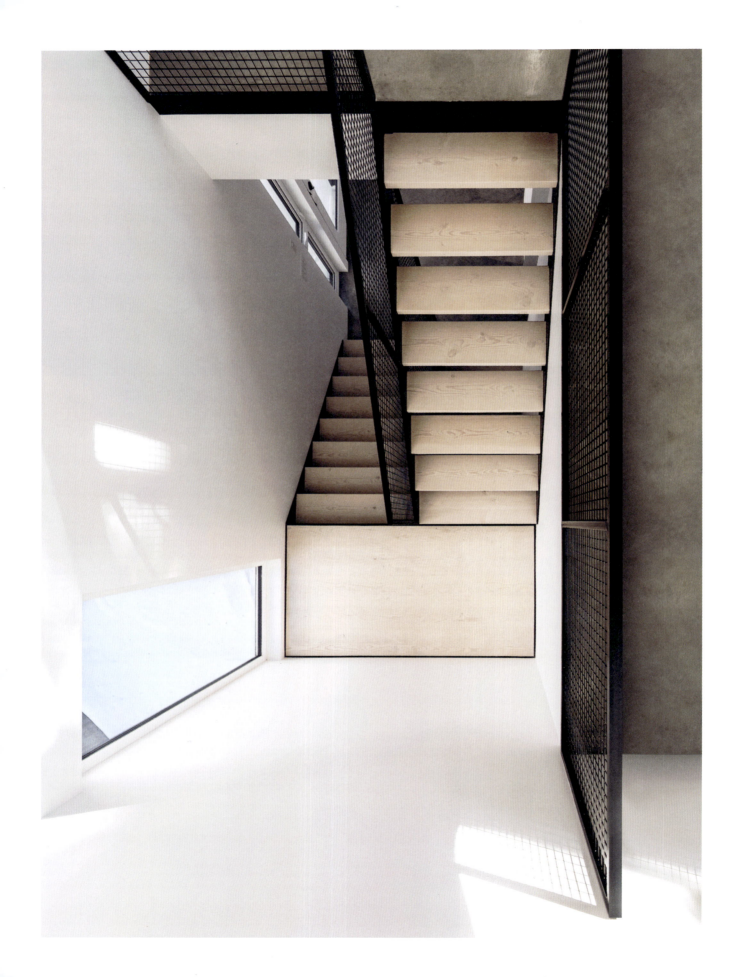

Considering the brief to "bring family members together and connect them to the boundless surrounding natural landscape", designer Bassett and architect Tyl, reversed the convention for an internal floor plan, placing the kitchen and living room on the upper level to take full advantage of the views and retreat-like experience.

"An open and generous common space is situated on the upper floor composing a quiet gathering space among the surrounding and seemingly endless layers of Douglas fir and cedar treetops," says Bassett. "From the cabin's upper-level balcony, the uninterrupted panoramic views of the Columbia River and wetlands emphasise the overall rural context."

The master suite and guest bedroom are located on the middle level, while a lock-off suite, ski gear room and garage are on the lower level. The sloping nature of the site allows for the building to have two distinct entrances, one to the lower gear area and one to a private back patio.

The architectural design and overall material palette were inspired by the cabin's natural surroundings. "We employed an uncomplicated and rudimental palette of wood, concrete and metal both on the exterior and interior," says Bassett. "The reverse roof construction provided the opportunity to showcase the substantial Douglas fir rafters paired with plywood to compose the upper-level ceiling."

Industrial materials such as concrete floors and black powder-coated metal are featured throughout and are warmed by the addition of wood millwork and furniture. Neutral interior finishes were used to maintain a simple chromatic palette and highlight the bold colours of the site's natural flora.

The result is one family's attempt to work collaboratively to lay down roots for their future in producing a sophisticated yet simple structure. "Through a solid foundation, and clever design, this humble property provides an innate sense of security, which in turn mimics nature's ability to both conceal and reveal its essence through the changing seasons," says Bassett.

> "The brief was to bring family members together and connect them to the boundless surrounding natural landscape."
>
> —JENNIFER BASSETT

Long Compton, Warwickshire, United Kingdom

DUTCH BARN

Designed as a transformative getaway for creative professionals looking to reconnect with nature, Dutch Barn is a converted agricultural building set on a 5.6-hectare (14-acre) site in the heart of the English countryside.

The owners of the property, Laura and David Johnston, founders of London creative studio Accept & Proceed, asked Carl Turner of Turner Works to transform the barn into a spacious country retreat as an acknowledgment to the site's natural beauty and agricultural history as well as one that would serve multiple functions: "We wanted to create a space where creatives and pioneers could get away from it all—refresh, rethink, rewire—in order to tackle the huge problems we face as a society," says Johnston.

The expansive two-storey home Turner designed offers its residents accommodation that features elegant minimalism and unobstructed views of rolling meadows and wildflowers in the rural Cotswolds.

"The design celebrates the pure form and industrial qualities of the existing barn structure with an architectural intervention based on simplicity and minimalism," says Turner. "This is carried through from the scale of the overall site to the very smallest details."

Striking in appearance, the barn features a curved roof and pitch-black exterior. "The external envelope has been wrapped in corrugated steel that lends a rhythm and texture to its 23-metre-long (75-foot-long) elevations," says Turner. "The matte black steel cladding unifies the façade and roof, simplifying the overall volume and reducing the appearance of the barn to its purest form when seen from a distance."

"Façade openings have been positioned and sized to respond to the barn's new use as a living space, giving the overall building a human scale," continues Turner. "Where original openings accommodated large agricultural vehicles, they now carefully frame views across the rolling hills and countryside."

"The matte black steel cladding unifies the façade and roof, simplifying the overall volume and reducing the appearance of the barn to its purest form when seen from a distance."

—CARL TURNER

Inside, the accommodation is arranged over two floors. At ground floor, the layout creates a large, open-plan space that has been zoned into areas for playing, cooking, dining and living. A double-height living space, featuring an upper floor balcony, forms "a moment of spatial generosity" at the southern end of the home, where there is also a chimney and two-storey glazing. There are seven bedrooms in total, six of which are located upstairs to make the most of elevated views across the scenic surroundings.

The design utilises a reduced palette of industrial and self-finished materials. White walls and sliding doors form a calming backdrop throughout the property, complemented by elements in pine, concrete, ceramics and stainless steel.

"Douglas fir pine wood was chosen for its warmth and rich grain, and has been used for flooring, stairs, handrails and bespoke furniture elements," says Turner. "Soft grey wool curtains with a metallic solar reflective backing illustrate, and further explore, the balance between industrial and homely qualities within the property."

In addition, there are 200 square metres (2,153 square feet) of scaffold board decking wrapping around the base of the building, connecting the interior with the surrounding fields and encouraging activity to spill outdoors.

Turner's clients, the Johnstons, live in London, so for them the development of the site and extensive upgrade of the barn building gave them the opportunity to get away from the city to explore county life. "As a family, it's an amazing place to go and spend time together, share experiences and explain to the kids our place in nature; what we need to ensure we protect," says David Johnston. "And as the leader of a studio, it's also a great place for my team to visit, to connect and talk about our plans for the future."

Some of the Johnstons' future plans include opening up the site to hold workshops for other creative teams. By embedding flexibility into the original design, Turner has ensured the barn would be suitable for its multipurposes. "Overall, Dutch Barn provides a calming and flexible living space, equally suitable for hosting families, mature groups and wellbeing retreats," says Turner.

"The design celebrates the pure form and industrial qualities of the existing barn structure with an architectural intervention based on simplicity and minimalism, which is carried through from the scale of the overall site to the very smallest details."

—CARL TURNER

Amenia, New York, United States

DUTCHESS COUNTY STUDIO

Located steps away from a jetty on a small lake in up-state New York, a compact, asymmetrically shaped, black-brick building takes in the rural views of gentle rolling hills and woodlands.

This simple one-bedroom studio dwelling is owned by an empty-nester Manhattan couple seeking a peaceful getaway from the city. Looking to retirement and grandchildren, the pair found 10 pastoral hectares (24 acres) on a lake in Dutchess county, but were at first apprehensive about full-time relocation.

To ease the transition, GRT Architects suggested a two-phase plan. "We proposed to start with a studio-type dwelling to let the clients develop a feel for the land before committing further, but first we needed to create a master plan," says Tal Schori, who was lead architect on the project along with fellow partner in GRT Architects, Rus Mehta.

"For this reason, we created schematic designs for a three-bedroom house, separate studio and workshop, swimming pool, firepit and dock," says Schori. "We then sited the buildings on the design layout in a way that they could share utilities, sized to serve all, and incorporated a common drive, septic system, well and electrical service."

Schori and Mehta kick-started the development of the site by building the studio first, locating it where it would have a view but not 'be' the view. Its construction features three rectangular components that overlap one another, with textured black brick walls tilted at the top to meet triangular windows.

"We composed three equally sized volumes in a pinwheel to create a 74-square-metre (800-square-foot) open-plan studio," says Schori. "Each mass has an identical roof, which sits atop a beak-like clerestory window. The masses meet at a centre point, marked by the pinwheel intersection of three steel beams but the interior is conceived as three subtly implied rooms, each oriented to a different view."

By dividing the space and creating areas for cooking, living and sleeping, and by additionally incorporating various levels, steps and built-in elements to perform many of the roles walls normally would, a separation of function is achieved within the dwelling. For example, a pull-down Murphy bed in the living space allows for overnight guests, while tall closets in the sunken sleeping space create some privacy between guest and owner sleeping quarters. The result is a layout that mimics a spacious studio apartment.

"The only 'true' room is the bathroom," adds Schori. "The bathroom walls are waterproof plaster executed in Moroccan tadelakt style and tinted a mushroom pink, and the floor carries the triangle motif forward with custom terrazzo tiles."

The studio is heated and cooled without the use of fossil fuels, using a radiant concrete slab and an air conditioning unit concealed above the bathroom.

Schori and Mehta chose a reduced colour palette for the interiors, relying on the complementary effects of pale timber-lined ceilings and wood cabinetry, white walls and pale grey concrete floors. Apart from the rosy coloured bathroom, there are also tiny gems of colour found in the custom-made terrazzo slabs topping the wooden cabinets in the kitchen. Another decorative and contrasting counterpoint to the overall light, bright and airy interior is the incorporation of black ceiling beams, a black iron 'clean-burning' stove used for additional heating and GRT custom-design dark metal light fittings—all of which subtly relate to the dark exterior.

Outside, the studio is clad in textured black brick, a material that Schori says "plays optical tricks depending on lighting, sometimes flattening the complex mass into a single plane". The roof is clad in natural cedar shakes, which are thicker and more durable than shingles. A copper trim adds an extra warm and welcoming element to the rooftop design.

"The owners have greatly enjoyed getting away to the Dutchess County Studio and asked us to proceed with other aspects of the master plan," says Schori. "The pool, dock and workshop have been completed and planning for the home is underway."

"Three masses meet at a centre point, marked by the pinwheel intersection of three steel beams but the interior is conceived as three subtly implied rooms, each oriented to a different view."

—TAL SCHORI

The studio is clad in textured black brick, a material that Schori says "plays optical tricks depending on lighting, sometimes flattening the complex mass into a single plane".

Toronto, Ontario, Canada

EVERDEN HOUSE

Located on a slim block in Toronto's Cedarvale neighbourhood, Everden House was designed by Canadian architectural firm StudioAC with a mission to be "impactful without being indulgent".

"The brief was to create a home that felt unique and personal to the homeowners and unapologetically contemporary, while still having cues to the traditional ideas of a house," says co-founder of StudioAC, Andrew Hill.

Inspired by this request, the StudioAC team developed a three-storey building that reads as stacked boxes, topped with a gabled roof that alludes to the local housing stock. Additionally, the peaked form was integrated into the shapes of certain windows and interior elements, creating a home that while dark and angular on the outside contains a light colour scheme within.

"While a gabled roof is one of the quintessential icons of a house, we were interested in elevating this phenomenon beyond motif to a spatial experience that defined a narrative throughout the project," explains Jennifer Kudlats, co-founder of StudioAC.

To complement the unusual shape created by the gabled roof atop stacked forms, the exterior façades were clad in distinctive black corrugated aluminium siding, selected for both durability and affordability. Additionally, the upper windows on the front elevation were covered with a mesh made from aluminium panels that were custom perforated and sealed. These sophisticated textural elements contribute to the home's distinct sense of identity.

The StudioAC team placed particular emphasis on creating a stylish, inviting interior, allowing them to be creative with their material selection.

"Our goal was to create a project that was impactful without being indulgent, but still within the client's budget," Hill says.

To complement the unusual shape of gabled roof atop stacked forms, the exterior façades were clad in distinctive black corrugated aluminium siding, selected for both durability and affordability.

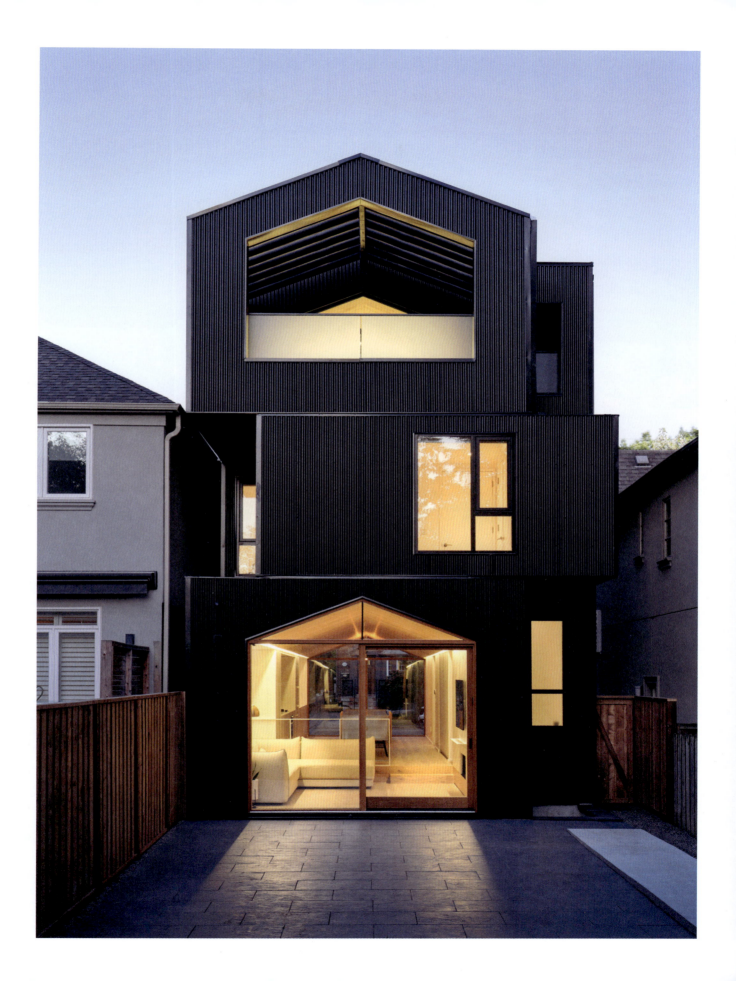

The ground floor of the house is divided into two levels, with a dining area and kitchen at the front, and a sunken living room at the back. The steps between the two areas provide a physical separation although the same ceiling height is maintained throughout.

"We wanted to create a sense of movement and delineation between the two spaces," Kudlats explains. "The living room feels like a grand space with a higher ceiling, yet still part of the continuous ceiling line from the front to the back."

Meanwhile, the interior of the house was designed with one eye-catching feature in mind: the peaked ceiling. "This allows other details to take on a secondary role, making them more cost-effective," says Hill.

The middle floor houses three bedrooms, while the top floor has a master bedroom suite and sheltered terrace, both featuring a pitched ceiling that follows the roof's gabled contours.

The materials used throughout the house are kept to a minimal palette, with white oak for the floors and ceilings, quartz for kitchen benchtops and white-painted millwork for the cabinets. Long LED strips along the ceiling provide a subtle yet effective lighting solution.

Ultimately, Everden House is an exploration of theme, motif and spatial experience that is both playful and serious. "In this project, we hoped to straddle the fine line between academic and explorative architecture while still being liveable, usable and timeless," says Kudlats.

"In this project, we hoped to straddle the fine line between academic and explorative architecture while still being liveable, usable and timeless."

—JENNIFER KUDLATS

Federal, New South Wales, Australia

FEDERAL HOUSE

In the small town of Federal, located in the Byron Bay hinterland of New South Wales, a black monolithic residence is cut into a hillside. Standing in stark contrast to traditional rural architecture found elsewhere in the region, Federal House displays a dramatic, bunker-like façade that encloses a warm and intimate internal sanctuary.

"At distance, the building is recessive, a black shadow within the vast landscape," says Kim Bridgland, who along with Aaron Roberts, both co-founders of Melbourne-based architectural firm Edition Office, designed the house. "On closer inspection, a highly textural outer skin of thick timber battens contrasts the earlier sense of a machined tectonic, allowing organic material gestures to drive the dialogue with physical human intimacy."

Within the folding hills of its hinterland site, Bridgland says the home "acts as both an experiential container for this place and as a conditioning object, consciously aware of its outsider status within the traditional ownership and legacy of this landscape".

"It is purposefully foreign to its Bundjalung country landscape and the deep time frame of the indigenous heritage in which it is located," he adds.

Constructed in black-pigmented concrete and veiled in black timber battens, the house appears closed and protected from the outside. However, the tactile expression and pattern created by the battens makes the exterior appear to breathe as you circle it—save for one side that cantilevers off a steep slope. Inside, views of the countryside are captured through the solid timber battens that are affixed to a wide verandah that surrounds the structure on two sides.

"The deep verandah allows for a shadow gradient to emerge between inner and outer thresholds, enhancing the sense of sanctuary from the surroundings and its variable weather conditions," says Bridgland. "It allows one to be outside in torrential rain and avoid the burning midday sun."

"At distance, the building is recessive, a black shadow within the vast landscape. On closer inspection, a highly textural outer skin of thick timber battens contrasts the earlier sense of a machined tectonic, allowing organic material gestures to drive the dialogue with physical human intimacy."

—KIM BRIDGLAND

Constructed in black-pigmented concrete and veiled in black timber battens, the house appears closed and protected from the outside.

The tightly controlled envelope of the layout allows modestly scaled living spaces to expand into a covered outdoor living area via large, sliding glass doors that can be left open to the weather or sealed off from it.

"This expansion and contraction of the interior allow shifts between the intimate and the public, between immediate landscape and the expansive unfolding landscape to the north," says Bridgland.

Within the home, dark wood and black-pigmented concrete are offset with lighter blackbutt hardwood floors, timber-lined ceilings and tan leather furnishings, while the three bedrooms and black granite tiled bathrooms arranged along the eastern flank of the house are described by Bridgland as "enclaves of withdrawal, rest and solitude".

Anchoring the project to the sloping site and positioned beneath the main living floor is a subterranean, all-black concrete pool. A glimpse to the still body of water below can be viewed through fern fronds planted in a double-height garden space positioned within the entry vestibule and lit via an opening in the roof.

"On entering the pool, the building becomes an instrument for the phenomenological," says Bridgland. "The mirrored horizon at the end of the pool draws one to its edge, and back again to the garden platform, its cavernous volume resembling more closely a freshwater swimming hole than a classic lap pool."

Fresh air is drawn across the cooler pool surface and into the upper surrounding verandah spaces. "This natural ventilation helps to stabilise the ambient temperature throughout the home," explains Bridgland, "and is supplemented with a ceiling fan for the hotter days of the year and a fireplace for winter."

Rainwater is harvested in a 60,000L tank. "The building utilises an aerated wastewater treatment system and includes infrastructure to utilise a PV solar array on a planned future storage shed," says Bridgland.

Serving the owners as a holiday home with the possibility of later converting the property into a retirement refuge, Federal House was designed by the architects from Edition Office to be a tranquil sanctuary for their Melbourne-based clients, while standing as a sensitive architectural representation of the firm's environmental philosophy.

Amsterdam, The Netherlands

FLOATING HOME

Built as part of Schoonschip, an energy-independent community of thirty floating homes clustered along a canal in a former industrial neighbourhood of northern Amsterdam, is Floating Home, an all-black timber house designed by Dutch firm i29 architects.

The dwelling is part of an experimental urban ecosystem embedded within the city. "The homes in this floating village make full use of ambient energy and water for use and re-use," says Jaspar Jansen, who together with the firm's other founding partner Jeroen Dellensen, was tasked with overseeing the project. "The site is energy self-sufficient, employs circular building practices and serves as a showcase for sustainable, communal living."

To that end, the house is powered by water pumps and solar panels, with electricity stored and traded with the national energy grid. A 'smart' jetty, that transports energy and waste, also connects all the households together and serves as a social connector where neighbours can meet.

To ensure design diversity, homeowners were free to choose their own architect—with the proviso that new dwellings must connect to the 'smart' energy grid of the village and observe the boundaries of each of the water sites assigned. An additional challenge was building on water to provide stability and buoyancy. i29 architects overcame this challenge with the use of a lightweight steel frame supported by an insulated concrete basement and by incorporating counterbalances in the design of the floor plan. The resulting house provides 525 square feet of indoor living space over three floors, which are accessed by a light-filled stairwell. Two outdoor terraces contribute another 120 square feet.

For i29 architects, an all-black aesthetic was an intentional design choice, as it draws the eye to the angular form, creating a striking anomaly to other nearby buildings, such as apartment high-rise and factories around the quay. The waxy blackened timber cladding wraps the exterior of the house and is continued within the outdoor living spaces.

The all-black aesthetic is an intentional design choice, drawing the eye to the angular form creating a striking anomaly to other buildings such as apartment high-rise and factories around the quay.

By contrast, the home's interior is light and bright and is characterised by white painted walls and rafted ceilings and blonde timber surfaces, mostly on cabinetry. This neutral palette was chosen to maximise reflected light and to act as a backdrop for plants and colour pops of minimal decoration.

In Floating Home, i29 architects ensured that the architecture and interior designs were "always intertwined and connected on each level to make a clear and unified experience" for the inhabitants. "All areas are in open connection to the atrium that comprises three floors," explains Jansen. "The layout is extended with a split-level connection to a loggia terrace just above water level. The interior and façade play with the views on the outside, so that views appear and disappear while moving through the home."

The main living spaces, such as the kitchen and dining area, are situated on the top level to take advantage of the light that enters from the large rooftop skylight, and for the amenity of an adjacent open terrace for outdoor relaxing. The main bedroom with en suite is located on the second level and opens to its own sitting room. Two more bedrooms are found at entry level, and also have a lounge area and bathroom. Both floors have access to an additional terrace.

"With simple yet smart interventions, this project is realised on a tight budget but still has a unified architecture and interior design that leaves a strong impression," says Jansen. "At the same time, the floating home is extremely energy efficient, eco-friendly and built with a small footprint."

The result is a home that is unified both inside and out, with a black angular presence that is offset by the bright and airy interior spaces to create a calm and relaxing atmosphere.

Arouca, Portugal

GRANARY HOUSE

Hidden deep within the forests of Arouca, in northern Portugal, is Granary House, a two-storey contemporary retreat that by virtue of its black exterior blends into its dark green surroundings. The house is located in a region known for its mountains and valleys, rivers and waterfalls, and is home to many species of birds and small animals as well as endemic tree species such as chestnut, holly and oak.

"Imagine falling asleep to the sound of a rushing river and waking up with the chirping of birds and sights to an opulent green landscape?" asks architectural designer Marta Brandão, co-founder of Mimahousing. "The architecture for such a dwelling could become secondary had it not been so thoroughly designed."

Replacing a pre-existing but dilapidated granary on a wooded site that backed on to a rocky outcrop, Brandão designed the new build as a minimalist guesthouse, which would retain a rustic ambience. "It is the perfect refuge from the hustle and bustle of daily life, where you can enjoy nature in total comfort while enjoying the pure visual delight it provides," she says.

On approach, the dark gabled roof of the building is distinguished by an unusual configuration of aged slate tiles, which were recycled and locally sourced from old ruins. Timber slats were positioned on the outside of a conventional post-and-beam timber framework, and have been heat-treated to blacken them.

Functioning as shutters, sliding black screens on the southern façade of Granary House cover wide glass doors off the patio on ground level when closed, and add privacy to the balcony above. When opened, they allow sunshine to fill the interiors.

"Cladding the building's façade in a delicate blackened timber slat, and its division into sliding wooden shutters to the south, transform the external envelope into a living and changing element," says Brandão. "For this reason, the house can sometimes display the austerity of a monolith, sometimes a changing face of a dynamic nature, enhancing different experiences inside. From the outside, however, whatever the positioning of the shutters, the composition is balanced."

"It is the perfect refuge from the hustle and bustle of daily life, where you can enjoy nature in total comfort while enjoying the pure visual delight it provides."

—MARTA BRANDÃO

As the new structure has the same slender footprint as the old granary, the internal layout of the house has been carefully considered to provide comfortable and stylish accommodation, which Brandão says "invites you to linger". It includes a kitchen, living room and en suite bedroom on the ground level, as well as a spacious bedroom and bathroom upstairs.

"On the upper floor, the sloping ceiling of the master bedroom, with its wooden structure and generous ceiling height, conveys grandeur," says Brandão.

The interiors of Granary House feature an abundance of natural wood, which is used for floors, rafters and cabinetry. The timber is complemented by beige earthy tones of micro-cement walls, thus creating an atmosphere of warmth and cosiness. Brandão then added a level of sophistication to this minimal rustic aesthetic by incorporating black metal details, as evident in an iron fireplace, balcony railings, light fittings and bathroom fixtures. Most striking, however, is a meticulously designed black spiral staircase that becomes a sculptural element in the living room without occupying much space.

Climbing the staircase to the second storey provides inhabitants with some of the best views and a new relaxation zone. A narrow balcony that runs alongside the main bedroom culminates in an outdoor terrace where there are built-in sofas and a small plunge pool.

"From these outdoor platforms, the sumptuous green panorama becomes the perfect backdrop for contemplation," says Brandão. "Meanwhile the sun peeks through the blackened wooden slats, generating poetic games of light throughout the house, favouring a permanent dialogue between the outside and the inside."

Functioning as shutters, sliding black screens on the southern façade of the house cover wide glass doors off the patio on ground level when closed, and add privacy to the balcony above.

Millswood, South Australia, Australia

IRON CHEF

Located on a leafy suburban street in Millswood, South Australia, a contemporary three-bedroom residence is shrouded by a black powder-coated steel façade. Aptly named Iron Chef to reflect the passions of its owners, a steel fabricator and a chef, the home's design reveals grand metallic and sultry black gestures inside, too. For example, a striking, black steel staircase and brass-clad joinery create distinctive features, while at the heart of the home, dark cabinetry in a large executive kitchen, fit for said chef, commands attention.

"Our clients wanted us to push them out of their comfort zone and so tasked us with designing a home for them and their daughters that was not only bold and dark, but also offered plenty of natural light within," says Das Studio principal and co-founder, Sara Horstmann. "While utilising elements of steel detailing throughout the home, Iron Chef was borne out of the desire to experience both dark and light."

Horstmann further explained that the client's expertise in engineering and steel fabrication combined with Das Studio's ambitious vision, which allowed for rapid, real-time collaboration and prototyping on many of the key features, resulted in "a true collaboration between client and architect".

From the street, the home's pitched roof form pays tribute to the rhythm of the surrounding housing stock of bungalows, rendering it sympathetic to its heritage context. "It was also important to protect two beautiful and well-established river red gums," says Horstmann, "especially since a quarter of the block was surrendered to a tree protection zone extending from the property's rear boundary."

In order to blur the boundaries between indoors and outdoors, Das Studio designed a series of glazed operable walls to open up the home from front to back, while the external materials of darkly stained, fluted timber and soft, sandy masonry was planned to wrap around the structure. Once completed, this created a seamless transition between the two spaces, allowing light and air to fill the home.

"On entering the home, a double-height void running the length of the home ultimately reveals a framed view of the celebrated trees, while allowing for the desired sense of space and connectivity between the kitchen and upper level of the house," says Horstmann.

But as well as light and dark, Horstmann says there is a sense of joyous expectation, too: "Hidden moments of drama and delight peer out from behind the black steel staircase to evoke feelings of playfulness and whimsy."

The sophisticated drama continues inside, with Horstmann overseeing material choices and finishes for the home's interior design. "The ground floor is defined by a rich and moody materiality, expressed predominantly through the ribbon of fluted timber lining that wraps from the outside in," she says.

"Hidden doors along the fluted timer walls conceal a dreamy entryway into the master suite, and another opens into the unexpected intensity of a deep green-hued powder room, offering a delightful contrast to the neutrality of the adjacent living spaces," says Horstmann.

The kitchen is a gourmand's dream and is distinguished by an immense white and grey marble island bench contrasted by darkened cabinetry. Travelling upstairs, the bedrooms, bathroom and treetop perch take on a lighter, brighter approach with warm oak joinery, golden terrazzo and a pop of pink.

Exuding a dark and moody vibe, this gracious home reflects the creative and detailed approach taken by Das Studio to deliver a bold and beautiful property to honour the passions of its owners.

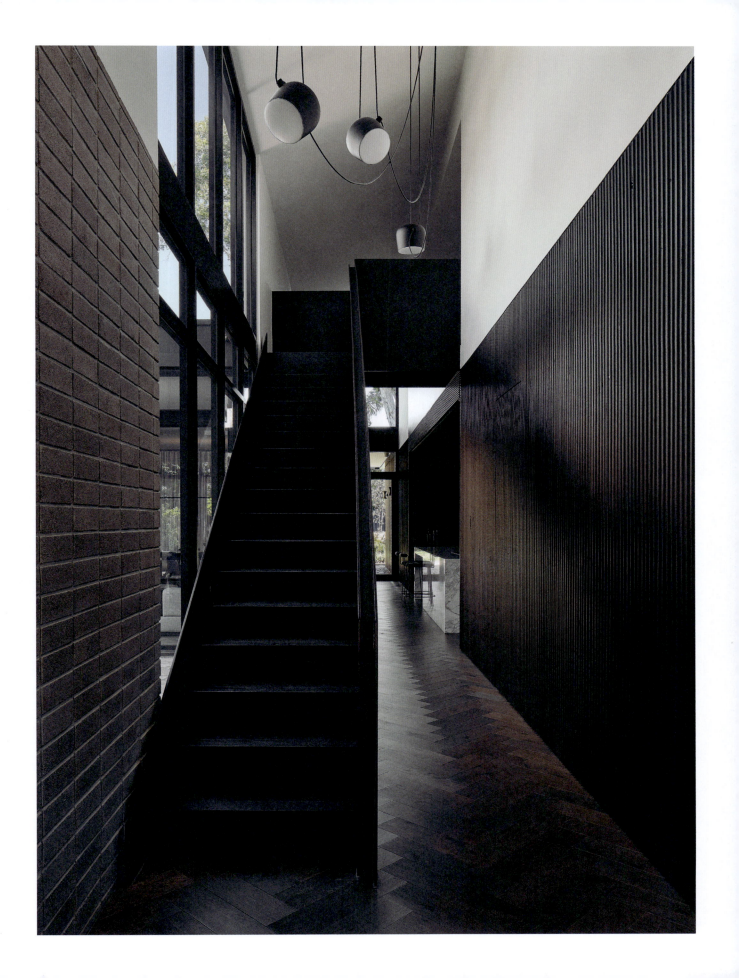

"Hidden moments of drama and delight peer out from behind the black steel staircase to evoke feelings of playfulness and whimsy."

—SARA HORSTMANN

"Our clients wanted us to push them out of their comfort zone and so tasked us with designing a home for them and their daughters that was not only bold and dark, but also offered plenty of natural light within."

— SARA HORSTMANN

Oberhavel, Germany

LUBOWSEE HOUSE

In northern Germany, five black gabled volumes positioned around a garden courtyard offer privacy and respite for three generations. Designed by Thomas Kröger Architekten (TKA), the elegant residence also allows its inhabitants to commune with the surrounding natural environment of forest and meadow. Additionally, the property is connected via a path and footbridge to the calm waters of Lake Lubow.

"If you step out of the forest onto the meadow, you'll see the five dark volumes grouped like a village to form a courtyard that welcomes you with open arms," says Thomas Kröger himself. "This intimate gesture of the protected square completely hides the neighbouring buildings, while the landscape design supports the path and view accordingly."

At the end of the courtyard there is a spacious loggia. This is illuminated from two sides and provides a view through the building to a deep front garden.

"The front garden is lowered to the street and entrance so that here, too, an intimacy is created through plantings and microclimate," explains Kröger. "Only three of the five house volumes can be seen from here."

TKA intended the residence to appear reserved and simply structured on approach. To achieve this level of understated sophistication, they had the exterior of the development blackened. This dark exterior created a perfect backdrop to the lush garden landscaping, highlighting the picturesque setting.

"Only the black wooden cladding, which is reminiscent of *yakisugi*, the traditional Japanese method of preserving wood, is striking," says Kröger. "This allows the green of the plants to shine more intensely against the black background."

"As you take the path from the lake and step out of the forest onto the meadow, you'll see the five dark volumes grouped like a village to form a courtyard that welcomes you with open arms."

—THOMAS KRÖGER

Upon entering the two-level, five-bedroom house, the dark, shell-like effect of the black, gabled, interconnected volumes is now replaced by a new intensity of light pouring in from floor-to-ceiling windows. The light bounces off pale timbers, light stone tiles and cream walls lining the interiors.

"One finds oneself in an interior world lined with wooden wall panels and light-coloured travertine," says Kröger. "Only the black handles of the façade and a few additions, such as a black kitchen and black-tiling in the sauna, create a contrast within."

The visual effect of the neutral palette is enhanced by soft jewel colours of coral, jade and copper. These colours are found on wall treatments, in finishes and on upholstery, adding further warmth to the interiors.

A seamless internal layout is achieved by connecting the five gabled structures via a central entrance hall, which borders the loggia and offers a view of a hedged garden. The ground floor compartment designed for the grandfather of the family is also accessed from this hallway.

As it leads to the kitchen and dining areas, the hall becomes an open corridor before terminating in a stylishly appointed lounge room featuring sunken built-in seating and a fireplace. Full-height glass windows overlook and completely open up to the courtyard, offering any one relaxing there contemplative views of the garden.

"Back at the entry to the home, stairs lead to a second storey, where there are working and sleeping areas for the parents," says Kröger, "while the guest area and the children's rooms are located on a split level. The sauna house is accessed from the outside via the courtyard. From there, the view extends directly towards the forest and the stunning lake behind it."

"Only the black wooden cladding, which is reminiscent of *yakisugi*, the traditional Japanese method of preserving wood, is striking. This allows the green of the plants to shine more intensely against the black background."
—THOMAS KRÖGER

Ota-ku, Tokyo, Japan

MURAKOSHI HOUSE

Murakoshi House is a quintessential example of creative Japanese architecture in the urban context. Bordered by narrow roadways on three sides, the angular box sits on a busy corner intersection in a neighbourhood of Ota-ku, Tokyo. Viewing it from the street, it is dark and compact, expressionless in features but beguiling in materiality and shape.

The site's exposed position, small plot size and the fact that one of the streets leads to a stream subject to flooding, initially presented Hiroki Watanabe and Takeshi Shikauchi, co-directors of architectural firm S Design Farm, with a number of challenges in meeting their client's brief to produce a stylish residential dwelling.

Clever planning and creativity offered solutions: "As the house would be visible from all directions, except the east side, we initially conceived it as a monolithic shape, closed off to the streetscape by a galvanised-metal exterior with minimal windows," says Hiroki Watanabe, the S Design Farm architect appointed to lead the project.

"In all, the design of a cross-sectional configuration, comprising two storeys plus a loft, garage and garden, together exactly matches the pentagonal shape of the site," says Watanabe.

The odd shape of the site and its size of just 73.92 square metres (796 square feet) also required Watanabe and the team at S Design Farm to maximise the building–coverage ratio. To this end, the foundation area was divided into three sections, with a small garden installed into the exposed triangular point of the plot and the main part of the house positioned to the back of the site. Between these two volumes, a drive-through garage was aligned to meet one of the adjacent streets for ease of access, doubling as a watery thoroughfare should there be any flooding.

"Additionally, we raised the foundation of the building higher than usual. By doing so, the height of the building was made closer to those of the neighbouring buildings to align the line of sight and make it easier for the form to blend in with the streetscape," says Watanabe.

Elevated on a base of pale concrete plinths, the exterior of the house is almost completely wrapped in charcoal-black metal-cladding, with only three windows, which are located on the southern façade.

"As the house would be visible from all directions, except the east side, we initially conceived as it as a monolithic shape, closed off to the streetscape by a galvanised-metal exterior with minimal windows."

—HIROKI WATANABE

Elevated on a base of pale concrete plinths, the exterior of the house is almost completely wrapped in charcoal-black metal-cladding, with only three windows, which are located on the southern façade. Although not visible from the street, the internal structure is made of wood and it is so well insulated that the homeowners rarely require heating.

To allow for natural light and the flow of fresh air while ensuring privacy, Watanabe's design of Murakoshi House features a large opening in the roof to create an atrium. This sits atop the garden courtyard on the ground level, with the two main levels separated by an open metal grid, which affords cross ventilation from above or below. Additionally, the metal grid offers a triangle of outdoor space for plants and further privacy to its adjacent indoor living area. In addition to the loft, storage can be found neatly tucked away on two levels, and there are separate rooms for the bathroom, laundry and kitchen.

"The trapezoidal living and dining room has a visual effect that makes it feel spacious for its area, while the floor plan and internal design allows for the line of sight to the upper part of the external atrium to promote a sense of depth," says Watanabe.

Without being austere, a minimal interior design aesthetic features within the house. Light grey masonry complemented by blonde timber flooring and wood panelling abound, while pale autumnal colours of sage green, plum and mushroom predominant the palette in the furniture, textiles and other décor found in the cosy one-bedroom home.

"I thought about how to create an urban house that provides a comfortable life combining the two aspects of a 'closed living room' and 'privacy'," says Watanabe. "In Murakoshi House, our clients can enjoy their leisure time surrounded by their wonderful interior collections,"

Naegok-dong, Seoul, South Korea

N HOUSE

Featuring a contemporary black brick exterior, Naegok-dong House (or N House) in Seoul displays a unique daring. Not only is it markedly different to the housing surrounding it but it makes its bold statement by drawing on a combination of minimal and practical elements. It is also one of the few single-family dwellings in the public housing district of Naegok-dong developed by the Seoul Land & Housing Corporation (SH).

The three-level home sits adjacent to a large-scale apartment complex and is also prominently located on a busy street where the road and the entrance to the neighbouring complex meet. The challenge for Sosu Architects, therefore, was to create a house of sanctuary on the bustling site.

"Creating privacy in the urban context became a critical starting point for designing this home," says Mihee Kim, who was lead architect on the project along with Seokhong Go. "For this reason, an outdoor garden is located at the site's centre and this is surrounded by the interior spaces of the home."

The team intentionally created the U-shaped plan to wrap around the courtyard garden. Although primarily built of concrete, the home's outer black brick walls act as a kind of architectural armour. However, plenty of natural light streams inside due to the positioning of large bedroom and living room windows on the inner walls encircling the garden. This fenestration also provided a pleasant view of the garden's greenery.

Conversely, the building's exterior displays few windows, save for a deeply recessed balcony, which not only allows for light and ventilation to flow through the upper level of the dwelling, but also offers a pleasant view of distant forests and hills.

The curve of the building's exterior softens its block-like shape, and a strategically positioned perforated screen of bricks on the second level allows light to permeate a stairwell that was designed to follow the exterior outline.

Primarily built of concrete, the home's outer black brick walls act as a kind of architectural armour.

"The curved shape of the staircase connects each floor and gradually opens and closes according to the direction of going up and or down the stairs," says Mihee Kim. "The exterior screen over part of the stairs comprises brick stacking. This appears closed outside to avoid the gaze of passersby but allows daylight to filter through to the interiors at the same time."

The entry to the home is via a doorway at ground level, more or less under the brick screen, and leads to a hall and storage space and a guest room on one side with access to the courtyard garden. Directly opposite is a spacious hobby room, which has internal access to a three-car garage.

Climbing the wide and gently curving stairs, the next floor focuses on communal living. Open-plan spaces flow from a utility room and kitchen at one side of the U-shaped plan through to dining and living areas that open on to the sizeable outdoor balcony. Behind this is a large bedroom and one of three bathrooms.

"The spatial layout on this level was divided into necessary functions, such as the living room, bedroom and kitchen," says Mihee Kim. "It was important to the family that we created a lively place where they could spend a lot of time together and share activities. For this reason, the second level of N House is divided into functional zones used by all family members to create an action-oriented space considering each family member's preferences."

On the next floor, there are two more bedrooms, with the master suite incorporating a balcony facing inward and overlooking the garden, as well as a private bathroom and walk-in robe. Another bedroom is located at the opposite arm of the U layout, and between the two bedrooms is a large study space featuring built-in desks and seating.

Internally, a sophisticated approach is evident in the choice of white walls being complemented by the warm hues of timber floors and cabinetry, and in wooden cross-beams suspended from the living room ceiling. The minimalistic décor and finishes further contribute to the sense of peace within the house.

"Creating privacy in the urban context became a critical starting point for designing this home. For this reason, an outdoor garden is located at the site's centre, surrounded by the interior spaces of the home."

—MIHEE KIM

Olivebridge, New York, United States

OLIVE PASSIVE HOUSE

Designed with comfort and sustainability in mind, the three-bedroom Olive Passive House sits in woodland on a 4.5-hectare (11-acre) plot in Olivebridge, New York, at the southern edge of the Catskills.

It was conceived as a residence for architect Alessandro Ronfini, his wife and their family, who together had bought and camped on the site numerous times before deciding to build a simple gable-roofed dwelling near a pond, a stream and a mix of evergreen trees.

Ronfini and his colleague Daniel Kidd, both of whom practice at DEMO Architects in New York City, collaborated on the plan, including deciding on the most favourable orientation for the home. In order to maintain privacy from neighbours, the house was oriented 30 degrees southeast.

"We decided to carve a wedge shape out of the house on the south-facing façade to optimise light and privacy and to re-orient the view directly onto the pond," says Ronfini. "This also created a protected private porch on which to eat, read and relax."

The 'cutout' concept was repeated elsewhere, with another wedge sliced into the north-face for an entryway, and a deeply recessed porch and balcony were positioned on the western end of the two-storey home. The 'cutouts' were lined in a honey-toned Siberian larch timber, chosen for its density and natural water-repellent properties.

"The warm wood lining contrasts with the black standing-seam, metal-clad exterior and alludes to the welcoming interior," says Ronfini.

Although there were many months in the planning stage, the construction of the house took little time due to customising its pre-fabrication. "The house was built as a panelised system in a nearby workshop and trucked to the job site, where it was assembled, atop a concrete foundation, in less than three days," says Ronfini.

"The warm wood lining contrasts with the black standing-seam, metal-clad exterior and alludes to the welcoming interior."
—ALESSANDRO RONFINI

"We decided to carve a wedge shape out of the house on the south-facing façade to optimise light and privacy and to re-orient the view directly onto the pond."

—ALESSANDRO RONFINI

At the heart of the home is a double-height communal space where the kitchen, dining and living room are located in an open-plan arrangement. Also on this ground level are a bedroom and bathroom. Upstairs are two more bedrooms and a full bathroom. Above the kitchen is a loft with a home office that overlooks the social area.

In contrast to the dark chunky exterior, the interiors feature a neutral palette consisting of white walls, polished concrete floors and red oak finishes. There are delightful washes of colour, too, most notably in the bathroom tiles and fittings, kitchen cabinetry and furniture choices.

"We sourced and recycled many of the fixtures and furnishings," says Ronfini. "A unique one is the 1960s pink ceramic sink in one of the bathrooms, which we bought from a store in nearby Kingston."

While ensuring the home's design provided Ronfini's family with a beautiful living environment, the architects were keen to meet the energy-efficient standards set by the Passive House Institute of the United States (PHIUS). Olive Passive House not only received certification but also won the PHIUS award in 2021 as the Best Project by a Young Professional.

"This building works exclusively on electric power and consumes almost 80 per cent less than most homes built in the same area up to minimum energy code requirements," says Ronfini. "The home optimises energy efficiency through a series of key elements. Triple-glazed windows maximise solar heat during the winter, while the walls and roof are insulated with dense pack cellulose. The building is also very airtight, guaranteeing minimum energy loss year round."

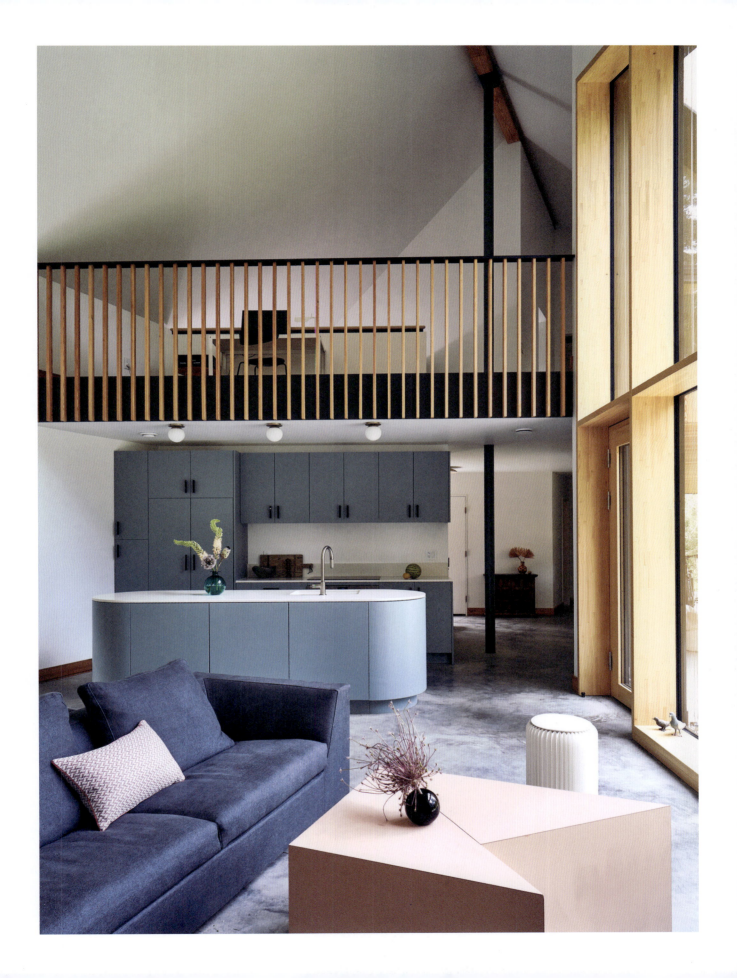

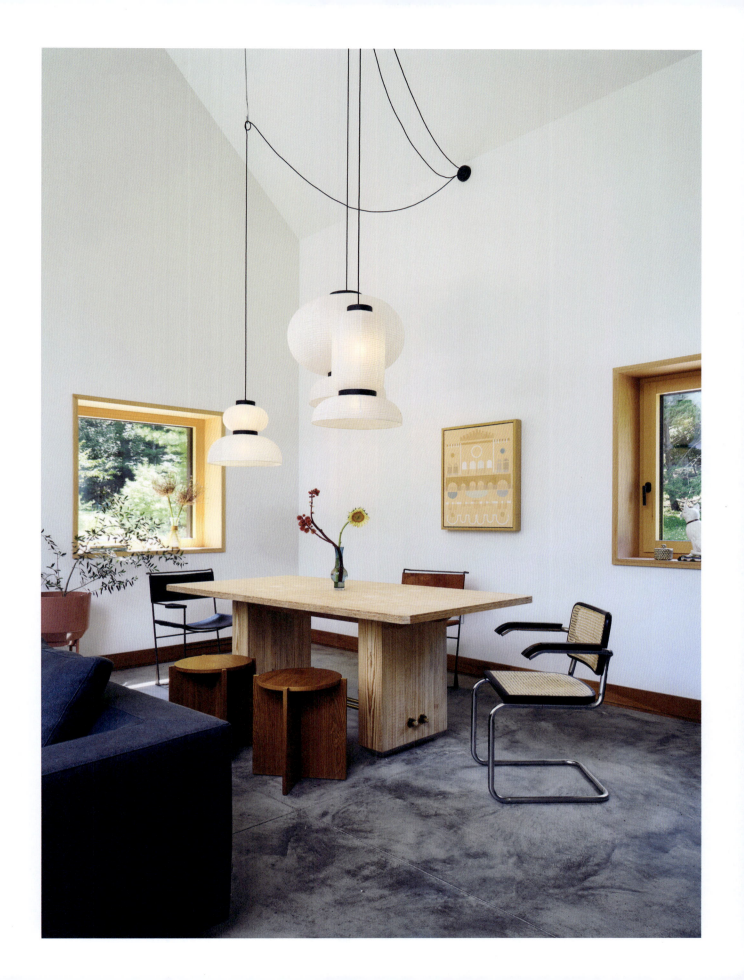

Singapore, Singapore

PERFORATED HOUSE

While dark houses are predominantly found in cooler climates due to the heat-absorbing nature of sombre shades, a well-designed black house in the tropics can provide significant benefits to amenability.

One such example is Perforated House, a sleek, black suburban dwelling in Singapore, a bustling city that enjoys hot tropical weather: high humidity, warm rain and plenty of sunshine throughout the year.

Designed by AR43 Architects, this private residential refuge absorbs sunlight and reduces glare due to its black colour. Like a deep, dark shadow, parts of Perforated House even appear 'hidden' by the lush, green vegetation that surrounds it.

"As most typical, small-block sized houses in Singapore are street-fronting and closely packed together with neighbouring houses, the brief was to design a house that would maintain a certain level of privacy for the owner, yet still being open to greenery, ventilation and natural light," says Lim Cheng Kooi, the project's lead architect. "To achieve this, the house was intentionally disengaged from a neighbouring semi-detached house, allowing for more spaciousness and natural elements."

Ventilation is achieved by rectangular cutouts in the exterior walls and roof, and strategically placed screens block direct sun while allowing a breeze to flow through living spaces. "The language of perforations was used consistently throughout the house as an architectural tool to aid ventilation," says Lim.

Passive cooling elements were also integrated into the plan, provided by extra deep eaves, openness in the interior design, water features adjacent to outdoor terraces and a lush tropical garden.

"The design incorporated solid off-form concrete, with multiple pockets of green spaces and perforations to control the level of privacy and light," says Lim. "Private spaces have been elevated off the ground, while gardens and landscaping act as buffers between the inside and outside, shielding the interior from noise and passersby."

The expansive open-plan interior living space contains a courtyard, rock garden and trailing plants and extends towards the surrounding greenery, blurring the boundaries between the interior and outdoors. "In spaces where more privacy is required, vertical angled sunshades were purposefully designed to allow morning light to filter in, yet limiting views from the neighbouring houses," says Lim.

An acoustically designed music studio was also built for the owner's jamming sessions and to house and display his personal collection of musical instruments.

Finally, a sculptural black iron spiral staircase leads to upper storeys and a rooftop open space, which was spliced from the typical roof form. This extends the garden from the family lounge to the attic level and provides a tranquil hideout with a panoramic view.

> "The language of perforations was used consistently throughout the house as an architectural tool to control the level of ventilation."
>
> —LIM CHENG KOOI

This private residential refuge absorbs sunlight and reduces glare due to its black colour. Like a deep dark shadow, parts of Perforated House even appear 'hidden' by the lush green vegetation that surrounds it.

Pajaro Dunes, California, United States

PLOVER HOUSE

Nestled into coastal sand dunes and tufty grasses, Plover House is a renovated three-bedroom beach house featuring a distinct pyramidal silhouette. The property is part of a resort community known as Pajaro Dunes, which lies along the shoreline of California's Monterey Bay.

"The owners wanted a vacation home to escape their city life and to provide an environment for their family of five to bond and explore the beaches and ocean," says Daniel Gomez, a lead architect on the project.

Gomez, along with Daniel Townsend, are partners in Fuse Architects located in Capitola, California. Together the pair closely collaborated with their clients to transform a tired and bunker-like beachfront dwelling that dated back to the late 1960s into a contemporary holiday house.

"The idea was to take the existing house and give it new life—one that met the needs and aesthetics of our designer clients," says Gomez. "The original house was very inwardly focused, with dark interiors and low-lying windows that you couldn't see out of unless you sat down."

Although the shape and footprint of the remodelled home remains relatively unchanged from its original, Gomez and Townsend wanted to take advantage of the ocean's proximity by removing any obstructions internally and by significantly increasing the size of window openings to provide framed views of the beach and surf.

To that end, the roofline was raised to provide extra room for expansive windows to be installed in the living areas, dramatically improving views. Within the home, ceilings were refashioned over the kitchen to capitalise on a natural light source coming from an existing skylight located at the roof's highest point. Additionally, the interiors were brightened and an open-plan reordering of internal space was initiated.

"The interior design is clean, simple and minimal to accentuate a light-filled space that allows the natural beachfront environment to be the focus."

—DANIEL GOMEZ

"White painted walls now allow natural light to disperse throughout the home from both the large windows and the central skylight, bringing light to all the perimeter rooms through strategic placement of interior glass partitions," says Gomez. "The interior design is clean, simple and minimal to accentuate a light-filled space that allows the natural beachfront environment to be the focus."

Rethinking the exterior of the house, which was originally, and entirely, clad with cedar shingles both inside and out, the architects chose to replace them with dark-stained Western red cedar siding for the walls and black standing-seam sheet metal for the enveloping roof. The dark colour effectively anchors the building to the sandy beach site.

"We chose a dark exterior to ground the home within the surrounding dunes, while selecting a contrasting natural cedar to highlight the point of entry," says Gomez. "The idea to choose black for the metal cladding was to create a 'contrasting canvas backdrop' against which the softly toned sand dunes and grasses of the natural coastal environment would be accentuated."

It is in this contrast between the built environment and its natural setting, as well as between the black exterior and white interior, that the success of Plover House's contemporary and empathetic design is keenly realised.

"The high level of detailing, both on the exterior and interior, captures a simple yet complex design that makes this project a testament to a successful collaboration of owner, architect and builder," says Gomez.

"The idea to choose black for the metal cladding was to create a 'contrasting canvas backdrop' against which the softly toned sand dunes and grasses of the natural coastal environment would be accentuated."

—DANIEL GOMEZ

Moganshan Village, Deqing, Huzhou, China

QINGLI HOUSE

Nestled in the picturesque village of Moganshan, a rural town located in a wooded mountainous region of Deqing province, China, stands a serene, inky black three-storey modern dwelling that incorporates elegant traditional features. Designed by HEI Architectural Design Studio, Qingli House sits on a sloping site that is backed by bamboo forests and is surrounded by tea gardens, misty mountains and running streams.

As Moganshan and its mountains are known for cool temperatures during the wider region's scorching summers, it has long been the playground of the Shanghai elite residing a couple of hundred kilometres further to the east. The village retains a country lifestyle with a mix of local inns and old villas built early in the twentieth century.

As Qingli House is positioned beside other buildings in the village, its design reflects the structure and layout of traditional rural housing. "We wanted to create an inward-looking building that is hidden, introverted and introspective," says lead architect Xianfei Peng.

For this reason, Peng and his team wrapped the layout around an internal courtyard and garden, which also accommodated the brief to provide both residential and homestay accommodation. "We learned from the practice of traditional gardens to use a high stone wall of nearly 4 metres (13 feet) to isolate the interior from exterior interference, and to open living spaces inward to create an internal world," says Peng.

Peng's team built four courtyards of different sizes, so that the whole building could completely enclose the courtyard spaces. The inner central courtyard can be viewed from various vantage points on the floors above, further enhancing the 'introspection' element of the design. Locally sourced natural pebbles pave the courtyards and some walkways, while larger stones are used in ridges and wall construction elsewhere.

"We added a layer of black painted anti-corrosion wood on the exterior wall as decoration, which can remind people of the weathered wooden façade of traditional Zhejiang mountain dwellings."

—XIANFEI PENG

The ground floor of the building is used as public space. It is U-shaped to ensure the mutual connection and independence of different functional areas. The second and third floors of the building are divided into three individual blocks as private rooms. Except for several tea gardens facing the west, the windows of the bedrooms almost all face the bamboo forest and mountains behind.

"In order to better integrate the whole building into the rural environment, we chose natural materials, including stone and wood, as the main base materials of the façade," says Peng. "Rubble cut by hand on the site is used to build the wall to make the whole building thick and stable and to form the foundation. Breaking the monotony of the wall, openings were positioned as entrances and terraces to interact with nearby watercourses."

The timber panelled exterior facade and walls were painted a deep glossy black, a feature that gives the house its name—the 'Li' of Qing Li implies pure black in ancient times. Peng says it was a choice influenced by historical meaning while also expressing a simple, modern style.

"We added a layer of black painted anti-corrosion wood on the exterior wall as decoration, which can remind people of the weathered wooden façade of traditional Zhejiang mountain dwellings," he explains. "Moreover, the grey stone wall presents a dark overall appearance. This steady temperament leaves a feeling of being deeply rooted in the soil for a long time, which reflects the introverted appearance."

Although Qingli House is a new build, HEI architects wanted its scale and style to avoid the 'foreignness' of newly built residential buildings that Peng says are ubiquitous in today's rural areas. "Rather, we sought to realise the design in a more cordial and elegant scale that was well integrated into the rural land yet still arouse people's memories of traditional provincial dwellings."

> "We wanted to create an inward-looking building that is hidden, introverted and introspective."
>
> —XIANFEI PENG

Woolacombe, Devon, United Kingdom

ROCKHAM HOUSE

Elegantly realised as a minimalist low-rise black dwelling by Studio Fuse, Rockham House features burnt, black timber cladding that creates a striking textural aesthetic.

"Externally the building is clad in Shou Sugi Ban, the ancient Japanese art of charred timber," says Daniel Rowland, of Studio Fuse who realised the four-bedroom home overlooking Woolacombe Bay in North Devon. "The black vertical cladding strips help anchor the structure into its context with a sophisticated yet rustic confidence."

The layout and design of Rockham House also takes advantage of the unique topography of the landscape on which it sits to create a multilevel experience that offers stunning sweeping views of the Atlantic Ocean.

"Our client had purchased a restricted access plot of land, chosen for its breathtaking sea views," says Rowland. "Perched on a steeply sloping Devonshire hillside, this exposed, yet stunning location, along with planning restrictions, influenced the form, which evolved into a single-storey building that nestled into the site's gradient. The building then makes sense of the contoured site with the creation of three flowing terraced levels, dropping down the hillside, reflecting the surrounding landscape."

The levels were also used to divide the home into different sections, with bedrooms on the top, a kitchen and bar in the middle and a living and dining area that opens onto a terrace and garden at the bottom.

"Glass slots along the side of the house bring glimpses of the coastal views to the very depth of the building while naturally gravitating you towards the main living spaces on the bottom terrace that opens up onto the rear garden and the 10-metre-wide (33-foot-wide) uninterrupted sea views," says Rowland.

"Perched on a steeply sloping Devonshire hillside, this exposed, yet stunning location, along with planning restrictions, influenced the form, which evolved into a single-storey building that nestled into the site's gradient."

—DANIEL ROWLAND

"Externally the building is clad in Shou Sugi Ban, the ancient Japanese art of charred timber. The black vertical cladding strips help anchor the structure into its context with a sophisticated yet rustic confidence."

—DANIEL ROWLAND

Internally, the home balances minimalism with warm furnishings offset by beautifully crafted concrete floors and cast concrete steps, giving rise to a gallery-like interior. "The connecting triangle components of the roof further help to create a simple yet sculptural space," adds Rowland.

The interior design was devised by the firm's client, the owner of the property, Deborah Vos, who worked with a monochromatic palette. She chose black accents for doors, window frames and fittings to mirror the home's exterior, while placing large, framed black and white photographs to decorate internal walls.

Black was also chosen for the bar area adjacent to the kitchen, which features black in the built-in cabinetry and a glossy black countertop that sits on a pale timber island bench.

On the next level down, a central ceiling-mounted fireplace becomes the focal point of the mostly white living area, with a dining table along one side and lounges opposite.

The bedrooms additionally feature dark finishes but each has large glass sliding doors or windows for views and sunlight. "Charred timber slats are positioned over half of these to give additional privacy," says Rowland.

Melbourne, Victoria, Australia

SANDRINGHAM HOUSE

Under the canopy of a substantial oak tree, Sandringham House is a restrained and sophisticated black residence located in a bayside suburb of Melbourne, Australia. Deliberately recessive in nature, the minimal black-clad pavilion is nestled into the site with the large oak becoming the focal point from the street.

The brief from the clients—a young family of four—was simple, says principal architect Ben Ellul of Ellul Architecture. The house needed to be light-filled, robust and discreet. "The clients also wanted a sense of privacy and security from the street without feeling cut off from the outside world," Ellul says. "As such, the house became a sanctuary for them."

From the outside, the single-storey residence gives little away. The uniformly black façade, consisting of a mix of vertical cladding and battens, envelopes the house and courtyard, with a single window breaking through the minimalist exterior.

In front of the black façade, a collection of native Australian plants fills the garden and spills onto the street, blurring the line between public and private. "Passing through the batten screens, which obscure the home from the street, you are greeted by another courtyard filled with lush, native greenery," Ellul says. "The plants offer a stark contrast to the austere black façade and allude to the sanctuary beyond."

Once inside, the true design of the home reveals itself. The floor plan sees a series of courtyards carved out of the rectangular form. Carefully positioned highlight windows along the central double-height hallway allow for light and ventilation to penetrate deep into the centre of the house. The combination of high-level windows with operable shading elements maximises cross-flow ventilation while moderating light.

Operable panels within the steel shroud allow the home to be opened up or closed off from the street at any given time. Screened courtyards also provide an additional layer of protection while connecting the calming native landscaping to the living spaces within.

"Deliberately recessive in nature, the minimal black-clad pavilion is nestled into the site with the large oak becoming the focal point from the street."
—BEN ELLUL

Interior living zones are connected to the rear garden and internal courtyards. "This blurs the lines between inside and out, extending the view and sense of space," Ellul says.

There are no steel beams in the house, so in order to achieve structural simplicity the capacity of the timber members dictated the size of the rooms. The master suite and study face onto the private entrance courtyard, providing a secluded calming outlook. "The client's initial brief included a retreat, playroom and guest bedroom," says Ellul. "In order to minimise the footprint, however, these were consolidated into a large multipurpose room, orientated north and connected to the central decked courtyard." For all the bedrooms, built-in robes were integrated into the circulation space to maximise bedroom size. The master suite includes a private bathroom, while a shared bathroom split into dual rooms allows multiple users.

Robust and honest materials were selected to be low maintenance and cost-effective, with longevity in mind. Black-fibre cement cladding was chosen for this reason. To elevate this humble material, the detailing was carefully workshopped with the builder Jada Homes.

The impenetrable black façade that protects the home from the outside, is replaced with warmth and colour within. Kitchen cabinetry references the black exterior, but is softened by a eucalyptus-toned green timber wall. The feature wall conceals several doorways along the hall leading into various rooms. "As a contrast to the black cladding elements, the interiors feature a colour palette of soft green tones inspired by the Australian landscape," explains Ellul.

In addition to the privacy created by the refined architectural form, this colouring creates a sense of serenity within the home, offering the family an elegant and harmonious residence.

"As a contrast to the black cladding elements, the interiors feature a colour palette of soft green tones inspired by the Australian landscape."

—BEN ELLUL

Isle of Tiree, Scotland, United Kingdom

TAIGH NA TRÀIGH

An imposing dark residence located on the rocky shoreline on the Isle of Tiree, off the west coast of Scotland, is notable not only for its monumental appearance but also because the ruins of an old stone cowshed, known as a 'byre', have been integrated into its foundation walls.

Designed by architectural firm Denizen Works, the four-bedroom home commands sweeping views of the sea from its elevated position on the southeast tip of the island, which looks east towards the mainland over the Isle of Mull.

Named Taigh na Tràigh and situated close to the township of Mannal, the house sits on land scattered with various farm buildings and ruins. These agricultural relics influenced the architect's formal organisation of the house, which resulted in two wings connected by a glazed link. With an intentional layout fit for purpose, sleeping quarters have been located in a restored building at the rear of the property while the new structure mostly contains living rooms.

"It is essentially a house of two gables," says lead architect and director of Denizen Works, Murray Kerr. "The residence nestles into the rebuilt stone walls, which drive the main architectural expression of the building. On approach, you enter through the stone gable into a courtyard garden from where you are presented with a framed view of Hynish to the south and a row of lighthouse cottages."

To create this expression in the new main building, Kerr copied the volume of the byre. "We slid it out beyond the old boundary wall and lifted it up to create the negative gable form," he says.

This allowed Kerr to install expansive floor-to-ceiling windows in the new structure to frame the ocean view, flooding the living areas with natural light. "Looking out from the main living space brings you close to the sea, creating a feeling like being on the prow of a ferry," he says.

The monolithic appearance of the main volume is entirely due to it being wrapped in black tar-coated roofing, which curves down, almost touching the ground.

The two wings are finished with materials and elements typical of Tiree, such as "stone walls, timber cladding, pebbledash render and bitumen in both sheet and corrugated forms", referencing the local vernacular of traditional blackhouses and cottages on the island.

However, the monolithic appearance of the main volume is entirely due to it being wrapped in black tar-coated roofing, which curves down, almost touching the ground. This gives a sense that the upper section of the dwelling hovers over the glazed walls of the living space. Kerr describes this wing as being "almost religious in scale", which is particularly evident at night when the well-lit interiors turn the black-clad dwelling into a luminous citadel beaming its position from atop the rocky coast.

The structure has also been designed to provide warmth and protection from inclement weather: "Constructed from a bespoke timber and a structural insulated panel kit, the house is highly insulated with heating provided through an air source heat pump," says Kerr.

A huge dormer window perforates the dominant form of the black roof, giving inhabitants a sweeping view of the coast from a master bedroom on the upper level of the new wing. Elsewhere, smaller windows frame views of the landscape. As well as the master suite with en suite bathroom, dressing room and study upstairs, the new wing contains a kitchen and utility space, dining table and the main living room.

"Sitting at right angles to the new wing is a restored building, which contains three bedrooms and two bathrooms with views out to sea and to the east to take advantage of the morning sun," says Kerr. "The ceilings of these spaces are subtly curved creating a contrast between the low-pitched roof outside."

Kerr created a tonal contrast to the exterior by featuring exposed timber framing, white walls and stone floors inside. These interior design elements combine with the double-height windows to enhance one of the most important features of Taigh na Tràigh—the dramatic views of the cliffs and ocean—while providing the property with a modern expression.

"Looking out from the main living space brings you close to the sea, creating a feeling like being on the prow of a ferry."

—MURRAY KERR

Chachoengsao, Bangkok, Thailand

VILLA BACKYARD

Designed as a family residence by TOUCH Architect, Villa Backyard features dramatic black geometry, which is most obviously apparent in the acutely angled roofline that continues down to cantilever over an artificial pond. The striking triangular shape of this house in Chachoengsao, east of Bangkok, allows torrents of water from tropical downpours to be quickly channelled into the pond while the structure's open framework increases natural ventilation.

"The man-made pond on-site was designed to serve as an atmospheric visualisation and relaxation of all senses," says Parpis Leelaniramol, a lead architect on the project. "It is to be used for water consumption as well but as the property is located in a region near the Gulf of Thailand where there is an excessive level of soil salinity and this can impact water quality, we needed to ensure a constant supply of fresh water."

To address this issue, the firm's co-founders and lead architects, Setthakarn Yangderm and Parpis Leelaniramol, adhered to the design dictum 'form follows function' and sought to solve the salinity problem by directing the frequent downpours into the pond via the dwelling's architectural shape.

"Originally the saline soil caused brackish water in the pond and could no longer be used for drinking, household use, or even agricultural use, so we needed to alter this low biodiversity water into freshwater," says Parpis Leelaniramol. "One way was to channel rainwater to dilute the existing water in the pond via our design. As we considered architecture to be part of this water treatment process, the shape and approach of our design had to support this development."

"The design originated by taking a simple cube that was diagonally slashed in half to provide a large, slanted, cantilevered surface to act as a roof and wall for draining water," says Parpis Leelaniramol of the wedge-like design that was eventually settled on for the home. "Additionally, this shape also had to incorporate all the functions of a single-family residence within a small, affordable and useful house, as well as adhere to sustainability principles."

The exterior of the triangular structure presents as a black geometric form but due to the openness of the design, the pale wood flooring and concrete panel interiors are visible, too, providing a welcome visual contrast.

The architects were also tasked with providing their clients with a low-cost, easy build. "For quick and easy installation, we chose a durable lightweight steel structure with an asphalt shingle roof to aid in water drainage," explains Parpis Leelaniramol. "Steel grating was applied for a cantilevered outdoor terrace so as to allow rainwater to fall directly into the pond. The grate also increases ventilation, cooling the air as it rises to the floor above, reducing humidity and water evaporation."

To promote shade and reduce heat, the architects installed black aluminium trellis screens externally. "The screens are not only durable, low maintenance and a long-lasting material, but can easily be re-positioned because of a clip-lock installation system."

The exterior of the triangular structure presents as a black geometric form but due to the openness of the design, the pale wood flooring and concrete panel interiors are visible, too, providing a welcome visual contrast. "The open-plan living space serves multipurposes, such as family gathering, dining and extension sleeping areas, thereby connecting both private and communal areas," explains Leelaniramol.

Entry to the single-level home reveals the soaring height of the structure. Immediately to the right, the layout contains a bathroom, walk-in closet and private bedroom; to the left is the combined kitchen and living area.

A large outdoor terrace wraps from the front of the house to the grated steel platform, which juts out over the water's edge. To further enjoy views of the waterside location, the steeply sloped roof plane hangs over the terrace to provide shade and is characterised by a serrated edge to optimise views.

"The design originated by taking a simple cube that was diagonally slashed in half to provide a large, slanted, cantilevered surface to act as a roof and wall for draining water."

—PARPIS LEELANIRAMOL

Gothenburg, Sweden

VILLA TIMMERMAN

Distinguished by a decorative lattice façade, Villa Timmerman is a black timber residence perched on a southeast slope close to the sea in a suburb of Gothenburg, Sweden. The house was created as a family home by architect couple, Andreas Lyckefors of Olsson Lyckefors and his wife Josefine Wikholm.

To partially finance the development, the architects designed a building that contained two spacious, almost identical, semi-detached dwellings. One was eventually listed for private sale, the other earmarked for the architects and their family. The only difference between the two halves is in their position. Otherwise, the floor plans are mirror images of each other.

Lyckefors and Wikholm were careful to include features to capture as much sunlight in both homes, no matter their orientation. To achieve this, they considered the flow of light through the structures in order to determine the placement of openings, such as windows, skylights and terraces.

"The stairs at the back of the house have large windows and glass roofs, which allow a good amount of light to penetrate vertically to the ground floor, and balance the large glass sections on the mezzanine level," says Lyckefors. "Light actually comes in from three directions, including at ground level, and there is always sun on one terrace or balcony during the brightest part of the day." Additionally, ceiling lights and a double-ceiling height helped create a home where the sunlight permeates the interior even on cloudy days.

The layout of each of the five-bedroom homes is intended to be adaptable to a variety of situations. "We wanted spaces that could be adjusted to family needs and function well during all stages of life," says Lyckefors.

To facilitate this, floor plans were drawn up to offer both private and communal areas on all three storeys of each home. There are bedrooms and bathrooms on all three levels, which can be readily converted to different uses, especially as family members, including children, mature. Open-plan living spaces are also found on all floors, and this offers a feeling of family connectedness while accommodating individual or shared activities at the same time. The first-floor kitchen and living area leads to a balcony—perfect for outdoor living during the warmer months of the year.

The internal staircase of the house is made of ash timber boards and veneers, creating a warm, Scandinavian ambiance. Due to its large steps, the stair treads also incorporate built-in seating, allowing for a comfortable living experience. On the ground floor and elsewhere, rooms are lined with ash panelling. This pale-toned wood feature is a common element in the homes' interior design, promoting a light, inviting atmosphere throughout the house.

The structure of the homes features a pre-fabricated wooden frame, which was assembled on-site. Its slatted timber-clad exterior was treated with protective wood tar and a unique blend of black and brown pigments. Lyckefors says the goal was to create a warmer black tone that could change subtly based on the light cast in different seasonal environments.

As an extra barrier to the elements, three grids of diagonal and vertical ribs were affixed to the outside of the wood cladding in a lattice-like design, giving the house its most attractive external feature.

"The grid was an experiment that proved to work well as extra protection against solar radiation on the façade and as a protective layer against the drifting rain on the west coast," says Lyckefors. "It also catches snowfall during winter, creating attractive patterns, which add a seasonal touch to the house."

To top it off, the roof is a combination of black-tarred wood panels and solar cells, all integrated flawlessly into the wooden roof with a carefully crafted detail.

The home's slatted timber-clad exterior was treated with protective wood tar with a unique blend of black and brown pigments.

"The lattice also catches snowfall during winter, creating attractive patterns, which add a seasonal touch to the house."

—ANDREAS LYCKEFORS

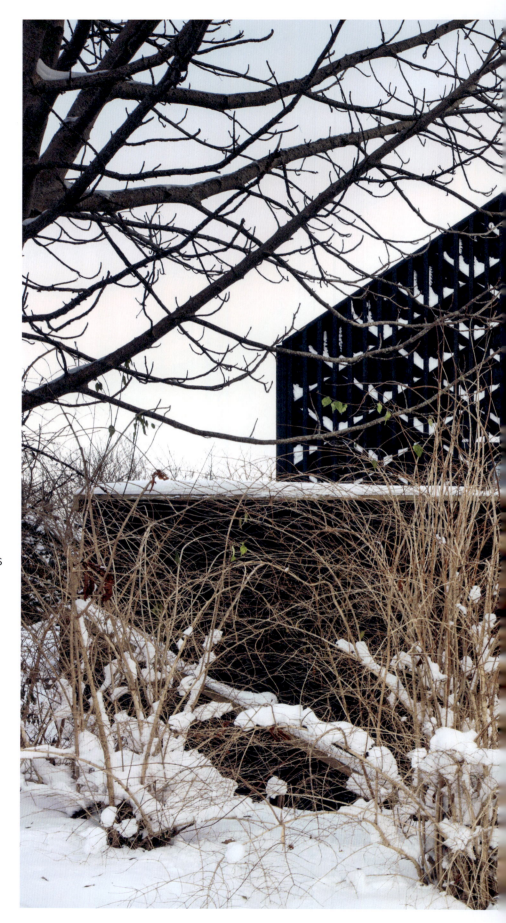

ECT CREDITS

AER HOUSE (PP12–21)

Architectural firm: Lesgourgues
emmanuellelesgourgues.net
Photography: Sarah Arnould

ARDMORE HOUSE (PP22–29)

Architectural firm: Kwong Von Glinow
kwongvonglinow.com
Photography: James Florio Photography

BIRDHOUSE (PP30–39)

Architectural firm: YCL studio
ycl.lt
Photography: Norbert Tukaj

BLACK TIMBER HOUSE (PP40–49)

Architectural firm: HAPA architects
hapa-architects.co.uk
Photography: Jim Stephenson

BROMELIA RETREAT (PP50–59)

Architectural firm: Plup! Studio Costa Rica
plupstudio.com
Photography: Robert D'ambrosio

CH73 HOUSE (PP60–71)

Architectural firm: LBR&A Arquitectos L'Abri
lbrarquitectos.com
Photography: Jaime Navarro, Frank Lynen

CASA BB (PP72–79)

Architectural firm: Elton Léniz
eltonleniz.cl
Photography: Christobal Palma

THE COAST HOUSE (PP80–87)

Architectural firm: staceyfarrell.com
staceyfarrell.com
Photography: Ben Ruffell

COLUMBIA RIVER VALLEY LOOKOUT (PP88–97)

Architectural firm: Twobytwo Architecture Studio
twobytwo.ca
Photography: Hayden Pattullo

DUTCH BARN (PP98–107)

Architectural firm: Turner Works
turner.works
Photography: French+Tye

DUTCHESS COUNTY STUDIO (PP108–117)

Architectural firm: GRT Architects
grtarchitects.com
Photography: Brian Ferry & Ithai Schori

EVERDEN HOUSE (PP118–125)

Architectural Firm: StudioAC
archcollab.com
Photography: Doublespace Photography

FEDERAL HOUSE (PP126–137)

Architectural firm: Edition Office
edition-office.com
Photography: Ben Hosking

FLOATING HOME (PP138–147)

Architectural firm: i29 architects
i29.nl
Photography: Ewout Huibers

GRANARY HOUSE (PP148–157)

Architectural firm: Marta Brandão & Mimahousing
mimahousing.com
Photography: José Campos

IRON CHEF (PP158–167)

Architectural Firm: Das Studio
das-studio.com.au
Photography: Anthony Basheer

LUBOWSEE HOUSE (PP168–177)

Architectural firm: Thomas Kröger Architekten
thomaskroeger.net
Photography: Thomas Heimann

MURAKOSHI HOUSE (PP178–185)

Architectural firm: S Design Farm
s-designfarm.co.jp
Photography: Koichi Torimura

N HOUSE (PP186–193)

Architectural firm: Sosu Architects
sosu2357.com
Photography: Kyung Roh

OLIVE PASSIVE HOUSE (PP194–203)

Architectural firm: DEMO Architects
demoarch.com
Photography: Chaunte Vaughn

PERFORATED HOUSE (PP204–213)

Architectural firm: AR43 Architects
ar43.com
Photography: Marc Tan, Studio Periphery

PLOVER HOUSE (PP214–221)

Architectural firm: Fuse Architecture
fusearchitecture.com
Photography: Joe Fletcher

QINGLI HOUSE (PP222–229)

Architectural firm: HEI Architectural Design Studio
Photography: Alili; uhe Studio
Interior design: Junyu Chen, Wenbo Da

ROCKHAM HOUSE (PP230–239)

Architectural firm: Studio Fuse
studiofuse.co.uk
Photography: Studio Fuse
Interior design: Deborah Vos

SANDRINGHAM HOUSE (PP240–247)

Architectural firm: Ellul Architecture
ellularchitecture.com.au
Photography: Hamish McIntosh, Rory Gardiner

TAIGH NA TRÀIGH (PP248–257)

Architectural firm: Denizen Works
denizenworks.com
Photography: Gilbert McCarragher

VILLA BACKYARD (PP258–265)

Architectural firm: TOUCH Architect
toucharchitect.com
Photography: Anan Naruphantawat

VILLA TIMMERMAN (PP266–275)

Architectural firm: Olsson Lyckefors Arkitektur
olssonlyckefors.se
Photography: Kalle Sanner

ABOUT THE AUTHOR

Susan Redman is an Australian journalist and editor with a passion for architecture and design. This has led to a notable career writing about homes and the people who design, decorate and live in them. She is currently the Homes Editor for *Sunday Life*, a Fairfax Media lifestyle magazine.

Previously, Redman has worked as a design columnist for *The Sydney Morning Herald*, *The Age*, *Vogue Australia* and *The Japan Times*, and has been a regular contributor to various home and design publications, including *Vogue Living*, *Country Style*, *Home Beautiful*, *Belle*, *Gardening Australia*, *Black + White*, Houzz and Domain. She's also written extensively about fashion, art and travel.

In addition to *Modern Houses in Black*, Redman's other books are *My Dream Kombi*, a title that celebrates the retro design icon and the fascinating stories of the surfies, hippies and celebrities who travelled in them; and *Love Shacks*, a book that not only features a collection of beautiful hideaways and retreats around the globe, but seeks to understand how people and places influence holiday home design.

Published in Australia in 2024 by
The Images Publishing Group Pty Ltd
ABN 89 059 734 431

Offices

MELBOURNE

Waterman Business Centre
Suite 64, Level 2 UL40
1341 Dandenong Road
Chadstone, Victoria 3148
Australia
Tel: +61 3 8564 8122

NEW YORK

6 West 18th Street 4B
New York, NY 10011
United States
Tel: +1 212 645 1111

SHANGHAI

6F, Building C, 838 Guangji Road
Hongkou District, Shanghai 200434
China
Tel: +86 021 31260822

books@imagespublishing.com
www.imagespublishing.com

Copyright © Susan Redman and the photographers as indicated 2024
The Images Publishing Group Reference Number: 1691

All photography is attributed in the Project Credits on pages 276–77, unless otherwise noted. Page 2: Kalle Sanner (Olsson Lyckefors Arkitektur, Villa Timmerman); pages 4–5: Studio Fuse (Studio Fuse, Rockham House); page 6: James Florio Photography (Kwong Von Glinow, Ardmore House); pages 8–9: Ben Hosking (Edition Office, Federal House); page 278: Mark Ryan (photograph of author outside Murakoshi House, Tokyo)

All rights reserved. Apart from any fair dealing for the purposes of private study, research, criticism or review as permitted under the Copyright Act, no part of this publication may be reproduced, stored in a retrieval system or transmitted in any form by any means, electronic, mechanical, photocopying, recording or otherwise, without the written permission of the publisher.

 A catalogue record for this book is available from the National Library of Australia

Title: Modern Houses in Black
Author: Susan Redman
ISBN: 9781864709667

This title was commissioned in IMAGES' Melbourne office and produced as follows: *Editorial* Danielle Hampshire, Georgia (Gina) Tsarouhas, Jeanette Wall; *Art direction/production* Nicole Boehringer; *Editorial concept* Susan Redman.

Printed on 140gsm Da Dong Woodfree paper (FSC®) in China by Artron Art Group

IMAGES has included on its website a page for special notices in relation to this and its other publications. Please visit www.imagespublishing.com

Every effort has been made to trace the original source of copyright material contained in this book. The publishers would be pleased to hear from copyright holders to rectify any errors or omissions. The information and illustrations in this publication have been prepared and supplied by the author and the contributors. While all reasonable efforts have been made to ensure accuracy, the publishers do not, under any circumstances, accept responsibility for errors, omissions and representations, express or implied.